INTRUDERS WITHIN

INTRUDERS WITHIN

PUEBLO RESISTANCE TO SPANISH RULE AND THE REVOLT OF 1680

by Louis Baldwin

The American Indian Experience
FRANKLIN WATTS
A Division of Grolier Publishing
New York / London / Hong Kong/ Sydney
Danbury, Connecticut

To Ginnie, with love

Photographs copyright ©: Laura Gilpin Collection, Amon Carter Museum, Fort Worth, Texas: pp. 2 (#P1979.125.134, Navaho Study at Mesa Verde (Hymn to the Sun), platinum print, 1925, 7 7/16 x 9 7/16), 118 bottom (#P1979.108.406, Laguna Indian Pueblo Interior of Mission of San Jose, gelatin silver print, 1938, 7 7/16 x 9 3/8), 137 (#P1980.35.12, Water Hole, Acoma, New Mexico, gelatin silver print, 1939, 13 5/8 x 10 3/4), 154 (#P1979.125.66S, Indian Girl in Ruin, Mesa Verde, Colorado, gelatin silver print, 1926, 9 1/2 x 7 5/8); North Wind Picture Archives: pp. 8, 16, 37, 42, 51, 59, 74, 102; Edward S. Curtis, Museum of New Mexico: pp. 25 (143728), 30 top right (144708), 30 bottom (160450), 80 (144511), 128 (143734), 132 (66549); A. C. Vroman, Pasadena Public Library: pp. 30 top left, 46 bottom, 96, 118 top; Arizona State Museum, University of Arizona: pp. 31 top left, 31 top right, 31 bottom left (Helga Teiwes), 31 bottom right (E. B. Sayles); Archives Division, Texas State Library, Austin: p. 46 top; The Bancroft Library, University of California, Berkley: p. 112; John Running: p. 148.

Library of Congress Cataloging in Publication Data

Baldwin, Louis.
    Intruders within : Pueblo resistance to Spanish rule and the revolt of 1680 / by Louis Baldwin.
        p.   cm. — (The American Indian experience)
    Includes bibliographical references and index.
    Summary: Recounts how the Pueblo Indians revolted against colonial Spanish rule in 1680, becoming the first group of Native Americans to expel their conquerors and reclaim their way of life.
    ISBN 0-531-11220-9
    1. Pueblo Indians—History—Juvenile literature. 2. Pueblo Indians—Government relations—Juvenile literature. 3. Pueblo Revolt, 1680—Juvenile literature. 4. New Mexico—History—Juvenile literature. [1. Pueblo Revolt, 1680. 2. Pueblo Indians—History. 3. Indians of North America—New Mexico—History.] I. Title.

E99.P9B164   1995
978.9'02—dc20   95-15080
                                                                      CIP AC

CONTENTS

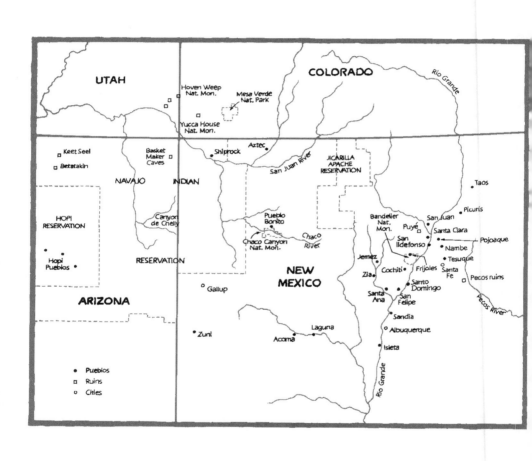

UTAH

COLORADO

Rio Grande

Hoven Weep
Nat. Mon.

Mesa Verde
Nat. Park

Yucca House
Nat. Mon.

Keet Seel

Basket
Maker
Caves

Betatakin

Aztec

Shiprock

San Juan River

JICARILLA
APACHE
RESERVATION

Taos

NAVAJO   INDIAN

HOPI
RESERVATION

Canyon
de Chelly

Pueblo
Bonito

Chaco Canyon
Nat. Mon.

Chaco
River

Picuris

Bandelier
Nat.
Mon.

San Juan

Puyé

Santa Clara

San
Ildefonso

Pojoaque

Hopi
Pueblos

RESERVATION

NEW
MEXICO

Nambe

Jemez

Tesuque

Zia

Cochiti

Frijoles

Santa
Fe

Pecos ruins

Santo
Domingo

ARIZONA

Gallup

Santa
Ana

San
Felipe

Pecos River

Sandia

Zuni

Laguna

Albuquerque

Acoma

Isleta

Rio Grande

• Pueblos

□ Ruins

○ Cities

AUTHOR'S NOTE

FOR THE PAST SEVEN CENTURIES, American Indians have lived in pueblos (the Spanish word for "villages") along the Rio Grande, the river that flows nearly 1,900 miles from the San Juan Mountains of Colorado into the Gulf of Mexico.

Three centuries ago, ancestors of the Pueblo Indians revolted against Spanish colonial rule, which had been dominating them for more than 140 years, and became the first group of Native Americans to successfully drive conquerors from their land—even if only temporarily.

This book attempts to tell the story of their revolt, including what led up to it and what followed it.

Louis Baldwin

FOREWORD

FIVE HUNDRED YEARS AGO, an estimated 30,000 Native Americans lived in dozens of village along the Rio Grande, the great river that runs through the present state of New Mexico. They were industrious, imaginative, peaceful people, with a rare penchant for minding their own business.

Hungry nomads roaming the vast plains that flank the river occasionally paid predatory visits to the villages along its shores in search of dietary supplements. Sometimes these raids were productive, but more often they were not. The well-established communities along the Rio Grande refused to cooperate in this free market system. Industrious and resourceful, the inhabitants of these villages made them nearly impregnable and would fight fiercely to defend their families and communities against armed invaders.

But against new enemies from across the eastern sea— enemies better armed, mounted on animals swifter than the great buffalo of the plains, and protected by magic thundersticks and powerful gods—against these enemies the residents along the Rio Grande were no match. One by one their villages fell to the invaders, and they were forced to surrender their freedom, yield up their stores of supplies, sublimate their culture, and toil for the comfort of their captors.

They were oppressed for almost a century and a half. And then they rose up—all the people of these scattered villages,

NINETEEN PUEBLOS

LOCATION

Seventeen in the Northern part of New Mexico on or
near the Rio Grande and its tributaries

Taos (Tah-os)
Picuris (Pick-oo-rees)
Nambe
Pojoaque
San Ildefonso (Eel-dee-fon-zo)
Tesuque (Tay-soo-kay)
San Juan (San Whan)
Santa Clara
Jemez (Hay-mes)
Cochiti (Coach-ee-tee)
Sandia (San-dee-ah)
San Felipe
Santa Ana
Santo Domingo
Zia (Tzee-ah)
Isleta
Laguna and Acoma (Ah-coma)

Zuni in western New Mexico
Thirteen Hopi villages in Arizona

LINGUISTIC FAMILIES

Grouped into Four Language Groups

Taoan
Keresan
Zuni
Hopi

CURRENT POPULATION

Approximately 55,000

bound together in rebel unity—and drove their masters south along the river until not a single one remained.

Of all the conquered nations of American Indians living in the Western Hemisphere, the Pueblos were the first to expel their colonial oppressors and reclaim their way of life. But decades of slavery had unraveled Pueblo society, leaving people unprepared for freedom and unable to recover the genius for cooperation that once was theirs. Unity fell victim to more personal, individual needs and to greed. Within a dozen years, their conquerors returned, this time to stay. The brief revolt was over, and the long-term future of the Rio Grande Indians looked as bleak as their recent past.

CHAPTER ONE
AN ANCIENT PAST

Newborn, we tenderly
in our arms take it,
Making good thoughts.
House-god, be entreated,
That kit may grow from childhood to manhood,
Happy, contented;
Beautifully walking
The trail to old age.

EXCERPT FROM A PUEBLO SONG, FROM A
TRANSLATION BY MARY AUSTIN (1868–1934)

THE STORY OF NATIVE AMERICANS living along the Rio Grande in what is today New Mexico begins in the wordless mists of unwritten history. About ten to twenty thousand years ago, during the end of the late Pleistocene Age, early nomadic hunters walked the high plains east of the Rocky Mountains, hunting the bison and the woolly mammoth, keeping one step ahead of the saber-toothed tiger. The land was cooler and greener then, chiefly because of the vast glacial masses still hovering not far to the north. This region provided a tolerable supply of nuts and berries and small mammals, as well as heavier meals of bison and mammoth.

Over thousands of years, the climate grew warmer, melting glaciers and nourishing the vast grassland in the south where grazing animals had permanently migrated for survival. Hunters pushed southward following the game and searching for more abundant supplies of plant life to sustain them. This period, which lasted more than 5,000 years, is often called the Paleo-Indian Era—an intense time of hunting and gathering food.

As the glaciers inched back to a frozen wasteland, leaving areas warmer, drier, and less generous, lakes dried up and green savannas turned into semiarid deserts. Mammoths and mastodons became extinct, and many hunters drifted north in search of smaller game that had retreated to the mountains and mesas of the Southwest. These nomadic groups formed loosely knit clans that hunted and gathered food to survive. Caves provided shelter from the blazing summer sun, from bitter winter cold, and from rare, usually brief, but sometimes torrential rains. Clothing was made of animal hides and fur, combined with a kind of rough cloth made of vegetable fibers. Simple tools—which were made from hard wood, animal bones and horns, and stone—were used for cooking, sewing, and hunting.

Sometime during a thousand-year span, from about 3000 B.C. to 2000 B.C., a primitive type of corn, or maize, passed among Indian bands and made its way into the Southwest from Mexico, where it had been cultivated by Indians of that region for thousands of years. In its new home, the corn did well where the soil was good, the growing season was adequate, and it could be tilled by committed, skillful hands. About the same time, an early form of squash was also being cultivated in the Southwest. About 1000 B.C. a hardier and more reliable strain of corn reached the Southwest from Mexico, along with a new plant—the kidney bean.

Because the introduction of plant cultivation gradually reduced the need to wander in search of food, people began settling down. In time, farmers created more permanent homesites in the sides of cliffs, close to their fields. They dug pits in the ground to serve as storage bins for corn and eventually built villages of large pit houses, covered by a kind of thatch roof. Before long, baskets were being made in abundance and the first forms of pottery appeared—then baked clay figures of people and animals. The ability to store food resulted in leisure time for other activities, too, such as decorating dwellings and clothing, and trading with neighboring people.

Centuries later, the villages of rude pit houses had grown into towns of three- and four-story apartment buildings, made of stone, timber, and clay in proportions that varied with each town's location. (One such building is known to have had 800 rooms, for both living and storage.) The people's efforts often were prodigious: millions of pieces of the flat, sedimentary sandstone from dried-up ancient seas were cut and gathered from surrounding hills and cliffs; thousands upon thousands of logs were hauled laboriously from mountain forests as much as twenty miles away. Some towns were built inside caves and under natural overhangs along sheer canyon walls. Remains of these communities can still be seen today, in Canyon de Chelly (Arizona) and Chaco Canyon, Bandelier National Monument, and Puye Mesa (New Mexico).

Around the end of the thirteenth century these splendid primitive towns, centered generally in an area encircling what is now northwestern New Mexico, were suddenly abandoned. Their inhabitants, the people archaeologists call the Basket Makers, or Anasazi, simply gathered their personal and common belongings together, including their precious seed corn, and left. Although the nomadic hunters to the north and east had begun occasional raiding and promised to become a growing nuisance, the towns today show no evidence of violent or even hurried departures. Although the tree-ring record (wide rings in wet years, narrow in dry) suggests a terrible drought from 1276 to 1299, towns with what must have been perpetual water supplies were deserted as abruptly as the others. And although the people's quarrying and logging may have been extensive enough to change erosion patterns and deplete their wood supply, this hardly explains such a mass dispersion of dozens of settled communities within a single generation.

Whatever the reason, the dispersion did take place, with perhaps most of the people heading for what some of them called the Great River, their earth mother's ever flowing breast

with its promise of unfailing nourishment. There they settled, in a long line stretching from Taos in the north to Senecu, near present-day Socorro, in the south, with important maverick communities to the east and west, from Pecos to Zuni. Their villages, despite great similarities, were quite separate, self-sustaining, independent communities. This dispersion and disunity was to serve them ill in the unprecedented crisis to come.

The people soon found river water to be fully as magical as the often inadequate rain that most of them had known on their high plateaus. They had no money system, but they knew the capital value of hard work, and they knew how to invest it. They soon learned the benefits of digging irrigation ditches, and before long the liquid gift of the gods was flowing through fields of multicolored corn and along patches of dark-red beans, golden squash, and smooth, round melons.

They did their planting, irrigating, harvesting, and storing by dint of much hard work and ingenuity, cutting channels from the river to their fields, which they threaded with narrower, shallower troughs. Beside each plant, each stalk, they dug a small hole deep enough to hold an individual supply of water from one of the troughs. And as things grew they tended them carefully, assiduously, laboring over them often from dawn to dusk.

This was the work of the younger men. The older men, having outlived their usefulness for such hard farm labor, took turns standing guard over the fields. Ensconced on the sheltered top of square, two-story towers, they watched over the young, maturing crops. Hungry birds were frequent vis-

Ancient ruins of New Mexico's native communities: cliff dwellings at Bandelier National Monument (A) and at Puye Mesa (B), and Pueblo Bonito in Chaco Canyon (C).

itors and had to be frightened away, for in hours they could consume the food intended to sustain a town for months during the barren winter. Small mammals, too, enjoyed banqueting at the expense of the human residents and had to be driven away with noisemakers or the barking of domesticated dogs.

Sometimes there were human raiders who had to be fought off because they didn't scare as easily as animal predators. These nomadic people from the northeast and northwest were called Apaches ("enemies") and Navajos ("enemies of the cultivated crops"). The less their hunting and food-gathering activities yielded, the more tempting these people found the food stores along the river. Their warriors were fierce fighters, skilled in the bloody business of hunting bison on the plains; their raids were relatively infrequent, however, for game usually was abundant in the lands where they wandered, and they had discovered that the otherwise peaceable river people could give a good account of themselves when fighting for their lives.

Tilling and protecting the fields along the river was men's work. By and large, women stayed in the village, preparing food, spinning yarn, weaving clothes, and watching over the children. The transition time each year was the harvest, when the men's heaviest work was ending and the women's just beginning. Both sexes gathered the crops and prepared it for winter storage. Even children were put to work. Although each family was assigned responsibility for a specific portion of the fields, the farmland was owned in common by the town, and everyone had a stake in making every harvest the best possible. This was the most pleasant and sociable time of the year, when everyone cooperated in preparations for the coming winter.

Once harvested and stored, food for the family became the woman's responsibility. When nature had been bountiful, storage rooms were brimming and caution could be relaxed somewhat to include sharing with visiting friends and relatives. Available food offered enough variety for her to whet the guests' curiosity with tantalizing odors and satisfy it with

18

palatable dishes. Meals were social occasions then as now; and the people enjoyed other people's cooking, and their company.

Corn on the cob was a popular dish, boiled or roasted over glowing charcoal. Another was hot cornmeal mush, made by grinding the kernels between two shaped stones, one large and concave and resting on the floor, and the other, smaller, held in the hands. From cornmeal, women also made bread and thin, pancakelike tortillas to serve as palatable foils for meats and vegetables.

Meat was less readily available along the river than in the higher country. But hunters occasionally brought in a deer, a sheep, or even a bear or a puma from the nearby mountains. More often, hunters had to settle for smaller prey along the river, such as beavers, badgers, squirrels, and field mice. The meat was eaten roasted or boiled, often with vegetables in seasoned stews, or was cut into strips and dried in the sun to make jerky, which was stored for future needs. Duck was available during the migratory seasons, and turkeys were domesticated. Pueblos did not eat their domesticated turkeys, which were raised for their feathers. Nor did they eat their dogs, which they treated like humans. They also did not eat fish, because according to a legend some of their ancestors had fallen into a river from a bridge that was destroyed by evil spirits whose magic had changed them into fish.

Pueblo diet was laced with vegetables, including lilies, onions, and juicy milkweed. The women stored dried pumpkin for use in pies and stews. From their food-gathering days, the people maintained a custom of community foraging. Every so often they would all join in a far-ranging, sociable search for nuts, berries, and fruits to enliven their meals. They would gather the leaves of many plants, from which they brewed teas, sweetened with a sugar extracted and condensed from corn.

The Rio Grande valley, which averaged about a mile above sea level between the northernmost and southernmost settlements, was and still is a land of extremes. On summer days the average temperature hovers in the nineties, though it drops to the sixties at night. In the winter it ranges from the high forties to the low twenties.

Traditionally, in summer most Pueblos wore very little clothing, mostly the conventional cover for the loins; the children wore nothing at all. But such attire was less than satisfactory in freezing weather. For untold generations they had been growing a high-quality, long-fibered cotton to serve their clothing needs. Some of the uncultivated but abundant vegetation, such as yucca, also provided fiber for clothing, and for rope and string. Animals furnished them with skins, hides, and fur, and domesticated turkeys supplied them with feathers.

Much of their clothing was quite beautiful. From plants, minerals, and clay they extracted brilliant dyes. On primitive but complicated looms they wove cloth of many colors and intricate designs. To this day, although their materials have changed somewhat—to wool and aniline dyes— Pueblos are famous for their weaving throughout the world.

The summer daytime fashion for men was simply the loincloth. In cooler weather they wore short skirts of cloth or animal skin, held up by a belt colorfully decorated and often embellished with a mosaic design of tiny multicolored beads. On the upper part of their bodies they wore ponchos, large squares of cloth with a hole in the center for the head. They wore no hats, but only headbands. Their legs usually were bare, although they had picked up the idea of buckskin leggings from the nomadic people of the plains and sometimes wore such coverings for hunting and on ceremonial occasions. In cool weather, their feet were bare less often, for moccasins were easy to make from soft animal skins and offered both warmth and protection. For greater overall warmth, and sometimes for greater dignity, they wore cloaks of turkey feathers or furry rabbit skins sewn together with thread from the yucca.

The people decorated as well as clothed themselves. Small beads and bells of copper adorned the bodies of some, anywhere from neck to ankle. (Like seashells, metal trinkets were a staple of the Southwest's primitive but far-flung commerce).

Most wore strings of magic colors or jewels of polished stone (especially turquoise) and painted their bodies for rituals.

The women dressed much like the men except that their main garment was a large piece of heavy cloth, some three by four feet, almost a blanket. It was carried on the right shoulder, wrapped under the left arm and around the body, and secured by a decorated sash around the waist. They also used paint, but on their faces only, not on the rest of their bodies. As for the children, they dressed like small-scale adults.

The ancient ancestors of the Rio Grande Pueblos had made their homes in caves. Caves offered excellent shelter and protection from the elements as well as from other kinds of enemies. They came in a great variety of sizes, shapes, and locations. Because the stone from which nature had hollowed them out was usually a relatively soft sandstone, or an even softer volcanic ash laid down several million years ago by enormous volcanoes in layers hundreds of feet thick, caves could be shaped and even somewhat enlarged with tools of harder stone. At or near the base of a cliff, they could even be combined with structures of stone or adobe, serving as the back rooms of apartments, as was the custom of the thirteenth-century people who lived in the Frijoles Canyon not far from the site of the modern "atomic city" of Los Alamos, New Mexico. Some of the caves were huge enough to accommodate whole villages, complete with two- and three-story apartment buildings.

When people began settling along the Rio Grande River, they devised new ways to make homes. Using clay, which was abundant in the area, they built structures that would protect them in this land of extremes. In the high heat and low humidity of this near-desert land, the clay dried almost as hard as rock, was quite strong under pressure, and was surprisingly rain resistant. Some of the people used forms made of double rows of upright poles, based on the same principal as the forms made of planks that we use for cement today. They padded the moist clay between the rows; when it dried, they had a hard, solid wall. Others formed the moist clay into blocks, which they could use in building houses very much as the stones they remembered had been used. Eventually these "adobes," later reinforced with straw, became the almost universal unit of construction along the river. Because of their splendid insulating qualities they are used to this day in New Mexico, much as they have been for centuries in the Middle East.

Apartment dwellings provided each family with a single room. A family consisted of parents and their children. Other relatives, such as grandparents, uncles, aunts, and cousins (all on the mother's side, for this was a matrilineal if not matriarchal society) usually lived in adjoining rooms, connected by low doorways. The rooms were small, about seven feet high and twelve feet to a side, their size depending largely on the length of the wooden beams brought from the mountains. If the living was crowded at times, it was tolerable, for the people spent almost all their daytime hours out of doors. Ladders abounded, since there were no exterior doors. To enter a room from the outside or leave it, one had to go through the roof. Inconvenience was the price one paid for solid construction, privacy, and protection from enemies.

Roof entrances meant that multistoried buildings were always made up of mounting tiers—a single-story row of rooms first, fronting on the community plaza; behind it, a two-story row; behind *it*, a three-story row; and so on. In general only the rooms in the first tier and at the top of the other tiers were used for living. The lower rooms were used for storage. Small windows, cut in the front walls overlooking the plaza, permitted a draft to enter and lift the smoke from the fire out through the roof opening. They also permitted a discharge of arrows when necessary, and presumably helped to minimize claustrophobia.

The climate along the Rio Grande, despite the usual thirty-degree temperature differences between night and day, is a pleasant one for outdoor living. Because it is a dry climate, with only a quarter of the Midwest's precipitation and with relative humidities that often drop to ten percent, housing is simply less important as a status symbol than it is elsewhere. Certainly Pueblos appreciated the cozy warmth of their little rooms on cold winter nights and during severe thunderstorms, but otherwise they had little use for them during their waking hours. Their standards were utilitarian, not materialistic.

Among the Pueblos, when a man married he joined his bride's family; if an additional room had to be built, it was added to her mother's section. Lineage was traced through mothers, not fathers. This tradition may have had its roots in a distant past characterized by greater sexual promiscuity, when mothers could be identified more reliably than fathers. By the fifteenth century, however, the people were firmly monogamous, their divorce rate evidently a tiny fraction of the rate in North America today. (This is especially remarkable because their divorces required only mutual consent, though with more importance attached to the woman's consent than to the man's. It was of course the man who moved out—not to his club, but back to his mother's hearth.)

By and large, the spheres of authority were kept neatly apart: the men ruled the town, and the women the home. Men hunted and tended the crops from which women provided the food and clothing. Men were responsible for husbanding the seed corn for the next planting season. They spent much of their time conducting the community prayer rituals, consisting mostly of singing and dancing in large groups, as well as performing the secret ceremonies held in the great covered pits (called kivas) that dotted the plaza. And, when necessary, they fought against invading enemies. Their defense measures (for which they usually had to work themselves into a frenzy) were effective enough to persuade their enemies to leave.

Children of both sexes were treasured. An expectant mother wore both her hair and her clothing loose as a sign of hope that the child would enter into life without hindrance. When her time had come, she would call a midwife (usually an older female relative or good friend) and have the baby in the privacy of her small home. If her labor was prolonged, or some danger threatened, the midwife might ask for the priests of the medicine cult to come and minister to her, delivering the child by means of heat, incantations, massage, and more incantations.

A birth, like everything else in their lives, was accompanied by ritual. A baby boy had his legs dipped momentarily into an empty black earthen pot so that he would have a deep voice (for incantations and perhaps for exercising authority), and then he was placed ceremoniously into the arms of his mother's father. A baby girl was laid for a brief moment in the hollow of the family's large stone for grinding corn, so that as a woman she would perform her duties well. Then she was placed ceremoniously into the arms of her mother's mother. The afterbirth was taken to the river (usually by the midwife, who was given a supply of cornmeal, ground fine, as a token of thanks for all her help) and cast into the flowing water as a sign of purification.

At sunrise on the fifth day after birth, the baby was named. A woman, usually chosen by the mother's clan or elder, called out the name as she held the child toward the rising sun. Until it could walk, the child was transported on its mother's back, securely wrapped on its cradleboard. (There were periods of time when men performed this task regardless of the gender of the child.) If a girl, the child grew up in the company of her mother, from whom she received daily training in home economics. She stayed at home, and her life was quite placid and uneventful. Or at least it was more so than a boy's.

For boys there was an athletic program. As they grew older, larger, and better coordinated, they imitated and even joined the younger men in their games. They ran a great deal, partly because running was considered a form of prayer that kept the sun moving in its customary path across the sky, and partly because it was critical for success in hunting, in sending communications, and in war. One running game, in which men kicked a hair ball formed and hardened with sap from the piñon tree, might cover a marked course thirty or forty miles long. In another ball game, players wielded sticks to hit a bag of seeds tightly covered with durable deerskin. Whoever burst the bag and scattered the seeds was declared the

Portrait of a young boy, taken by Edward S. Curtis at San Ildefonso Pueblo, 1905

winner. And then there were other games that gave them practice throwing stones and sharp-tipped spears and even arrows.

More important than athletics was a boy's introduction into the political and religious life of the community (those two aspects were, of course, inseparable). Between the ages of five and ten, boys were brought to meetings held in the kivas to learn an important lesson from the masked gods and the demigods called kachinas. A tradition of beating the boys, with whips of yucca hard enough to make them cry, was meant to force the evil out of them and help them learn how to bear their share of pain and hardship in later life.

As boys approached puberty, the ceremony intensified. They were whipped even harder by the gods, who they believed were spiritual powers from the underworld where the sun went every night. When the whipping stopped, the gods raised their brightly painted wooden masks and revealed the familiar faces of older male relatives and friends. At this point, the boys were given masks and whips and allowed to whip those who had tormented them. This ceremony signaled a boy's coming of age, when he learned what women and children were not allowed to know (at least officially), that the gods no longer left their underworld, but instead were represented in this world by men in disguise. Not that the gods were powerless on earth, for, among other things, they would severely punish any man who revealed their secret. Although the truth of the matter was generally known, it was never to be voiced.

One reason for the secrecy was that some of the frightening gods were useful in controlling unruly youngsters, somewhat as Santa Claus has been useful in more recent times. Each year the gods paid the children of the village an admonitory visit. They asked questions about their behavior during the preceding months. For some of the children the questions were very embarrassing because the gods seemed to know the answers before the children spoke. The parents pleaded on their behalf: "Please, give the children another chance; they'll be good, they'll be good." Of course, the children tearfully concurred. Then the gods relented: "Very well, another chance, but we'll be back next year." For the mischievous children this must have been a very sobering experience, which doubtless modified their behavior for as long as a day or two.

Pueblos obviously held the institution of the family in considerable esteem and took its responsibilities very seriously. If love can be defined as concern and care for another, their lives showed plenty of love, especially within the family. Whether this reverence extended to their Creator is open to some question; certainly their fear did. But their gentle affection for their common mother, the nourishing land, was an inseparable part of their daily lives.

However great each pueblo's similarities, they were quite separate political entities. Indeed, their separation and independence were to be their downfall. In such highly organized communities, a chronic condition of unlimited power by one leader might have been expected, but, if there was any dictatorship in these towns, it was a dictatorship of the overwhelming majority. The people were sensitive to signs of political ambition and apparently quite effective in controlling it with ridicule. Theirs was a government of consensus and consent, and no single individual had enough authority or power to contravene it.

The town belonged to all in common, as did the farmland that fed it. A council of elders allocated plots of the farmland to families according to need, with adjustments made yearly as needs changed. After these basic allotments were allocated, a kind of capitalism took over. The food from the family's plot was privately owned by them, and their success depended on their investment of time, labor, and intelligence. Similarly, rooms were assigned on the basis of need but thereafter were privately owned by the family, could be changed as necessary and practicable, and were allowed to go to ruin if the family died out. Personal property—baskets, pottery, grinding stones, clothing items, all the relatively little things of daily use—were just that, personal property. This kind of communal economy, lacking a money system, furnished no opportunity for the vast disparities in wealth that characterized other civilizations. Among Pueblos, everyone lived pretty much the same.

Members of such a closed society valued self-restraint as a virtue assiduously cultivated in oneself and others. Harmless eccentricity evidently was tolerated, but antisocial behavior was not. Emotionalism was suspect, and violence was forbidden. Personal ambition, including political ambition, was rigorously suppressed by general contempt, though a contempt normally expressed in good-natured ridicule.

The government was based on the natural clan system, and every family belonged to one or another of the kiva sodalities, or societies, that largely set the social, political, and religious tone of the river communities. In general, each used a separate season of the year for planning and organizing the prayer ceremonies appropriate to that particular season. There was good reason for the seasonal division of labor: the number and variety of ceremonies were much too great for any single group to handle, especially since tradition meticulously prescribed the words and movements in great detail. Because there were no written records, everything had to be precisely memorized from generation to generation. And because memories often differed and tempers sometimes flared, there had to be a court of last resort.

This final authority resided in the office of chief priest. Chosen by the other priests and elders of the town, the chief priest held his office for life. His authority was nearly absolute in settling disputed questions of ritual. He was expected, not unlike a Christian ascetic, to promote his own detachment with fasting and prayer. Uniquely, he did not farm or hunt. His crops were planted, cultivated, and harvested, his meat was hunted and trapped, his meals were cooked, and his apartment was built and furnished, all by others. He even had a house-keeper. All this special treatment was necessary because nothing of any consequence was done in the village without a ceremony, and no ceremony was conducted without his blessing. Because there was no delegating of this responsibility, he was a very busy man.

Once a year he performed the important duty of ordaining men to be priests, particularly the two priests of warfare and their dozen or so assistants (all of whom, both priests and assistants, served only until the following year). These were the leaders of the war society —an unenviable position, for the river people were reluctant warriors. Indeed, one of their war chants, sung before going off to battle, was really a lament in which the warriors bewailed their bad luck in being men and having to go off to war, leaving the women in the cozy safety of the home. Membership in the war society was a kind of punishment, limited to homicides (all those who had killed another, accidentally or deliberately, in war or in peace). Members could earn the forgiveness of the gods and of their fellow men and women only by serving a hitch in the army. Upon their return from a war, the warriors had to spend the better part of a week or two in prayer and fasting and in bathing body and soul in the cleansing waters of the sacred river, which gave life and could restore it.

Pueblos believed that in war they had everything to lose and nothing to gain, unlike their nomadic enemies, who went to war when hunting was poor and nuts and berries were scarce. A decision to go to war, always a last resort, was made in the solemn conclave of the chief priest, the war priests, and other priests and elders. Like all major decisions, this one was preceded and accompanied by prayer and fasting. If its urgency did not match its importance (as in the case of considering the necessity of a preventive strike), the decision might take two or three days.

Pueblos had neither a system of writing nor much need for one, at least beyond the simple rock carvings whose mysteries still provide southwestern archaeologists and anthropologists with much food for thought and dissertation. Their arithmetic may not have advanced very far, but discoveries in Chaco Canyon in New Mexico suggest that they knew a good deal about geometry without ever having heard of Euclid. And about astronomy, too, in which they seem to have been no more naive than the ancient Greeks and at least as knowledgeable as the creators of Stonehenge.

In other respects their technology suited their needs quite well. When and where groundwater was not plentiful, they had become the world's greatest experts in dry farming. They had developed corn, which is the only grain crop individually planted rather than sown and which therefore can be individually nurtured in hard, dry soil. And they had developed strains of corn unequaled to this day, corn with stunted stalks but full, rich ears. Where flowing water was available, they became expert in methods of irrigation. Their stone and adobe apartment houses were reasonably comfortable and solidly constructed, providing a good measure of protection from both elements and enemies. The builders knew the principles of ventilation and used them to good advantage, especially in the kivas, using both the radiant and the convective effects of fire.

They used large, beehive-shaped adobe ovens for baking bread, spits for roasting meat, and large earthen jars for heating water. Water could be brought to a boil by heating stones in a fire and then dropping them into water-filled jugs. The men used a similar method of heating water for their steam baths by pouring the water over heated stones in a closed room. Thin, flat stones were used for skillets by the women,

A

B

C

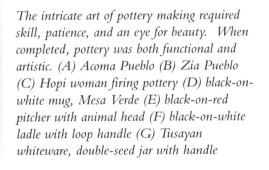

The intricate art of pottery making required skill, patience, and an eye for beauty. When completed, pottery was both functional and artistic. (A) Acoma Pueblo (B) Zia Pueblo (C) Hopi woman firing pottery (D) black-on-white mug, Mesa Verde (E) black-on-red pitcher with animal head (F) black-on-white ladle with loop handle (G) Tusayan whiteware, double-seed jar with handle

although sometimes a stone's tendency to crack when heated could result in a culinary disaster.

It was chiefly in things culinary that the people's technology shaded into their art. The women wove colorful baskets, of all sizes and shapes and of infinite variety and design. The weaving patterns were very intricate, with the vegetable fibers coiled so tightly that many of the baskets were used to hold water. The woven multicolored designs, some simple and others so complicated as to invite study, included both sinuous abstractions and appealing representations of favorite animals, people, and the kachina demigods. Similar designs graced the pottery, painted with yucca-leaf brushes and a kind of brightly colored paste whose base was the juice of the yucca fruit. Like nearly everything else in the lives of these people, the decoration of pottery, baskets, clothing, and walls was somehow ceremonial. They believed that decorating a pot gave it a kind of life, the degree or intensity of the life depending on the quality of the artistry. And apparently they did their best to give it as good a life as could be. Their technology was a gentle harnessing of nature. Their art was a gentle expression of nature. Both fit well into their philosophy of life and adequately met their needs.

They were an extremely religious people, in the sense that their harmony with a deified nature was ever uppermost in their minds. Their lives were filled with prayer. They greeted the sun in the morning with a prayer and bade it a prayerful *au revoir* at night. They prayed in their cornfields, in their vegetable gardens, and in their homes, as well as in their ceremonial kivas. They prayed at work and at play, before hunting and before battle, in their songs and during their dancing.

They believed in an ultimate being, most commonly in the form of the "Woman Who Thinks." This thinking woman, however, was rather vague and distant. Second in rank was the Corn Mother, or Mother Earth, goddess of the underworld from which she led the people's first ancestors and to which she welcomed those returning from the life above. She was the more immediate provider of life-giving things; but still more immediate, and next in rank, were the Two

32

Sisters, who had introduced to the upper world the plants and animals on which the people depended for sustenance.

"Our Father the Sun" was accorded almost universal reverence. Most of the people prayed when necessary to the young twin gods of war, who were characterized more by mischievous behavior than by martial fervor. There were spirits assigned to each of the six directions: north, south, east and west (approximately), and the zenith and the nadir. And there were the clown gods—the koshare—who enforced a measure of conformity through the power of ridicule.

Spirit, or spirits, abided in everything, from the gods through humans, animals, and plants to even inanimate things like rocks and man-made things like baskets and pots. Spirits could be good or bad but were never indifferent, and it took a powerful lot of prayer to win help from the good and to fend off the bad. The sun, of course, was very good—indeed, indispensable—but sometimes he overdid it and the gods of clouds and rain would have to be entreated for protection. And sometimes, although much more rarely, *they* would overdo it. Then floods of water from the sky would damage crops and homes, swelling streams and creeks into torrents on a rampage. Then Father Sun would have to be implored to restore the balance. Although the people were as close to and as respectful of nature as perhaps any other people in the world, the gods of nature often were capricious and unpredictable and distressingly unresponsive. Not always unresponsive, however, and so the people continued to pray.

Their prayer took various forms, often using analogy. In prayers for rain, for example, feathers were used because they resembled rain clouds. The material used most commonly for prayer was white cornmeal, the ancient American staff of life. The person praying would take some in his hand and breathe on it, making the ageless and universal association of breath with spirit, and sprinkle it like holy water on person, place, or thing as a blessing. Father Sun was greeted in the morning with a prayer and a sprinkling of meal. Priests, warriors, and hunters were sprinkled with meal, or it might be sprinkled on the ground before them. Sometimes a line of holy meal was poured on the ground during negotiations with enemies as a line of demarcation: "This far, but no farther." Occasionally pollen was used instead of cornmeal, for it too was a symbol of life.

Neither cornmeal nor pollen lasted very long after a sprinkling, so for a more durable form of prayer the people used prayer sticks, which served somewhat the same function as the original Christmas tree or the lighted holy candles in Roman Catholic churches, symbolizing the prayers associated with them for as long as they lasted. They were carved out of wood and were brightly decorated with colored paints: red from sandstone imbued by iron, yellow from the ochre in eroded canyon cliffsides, green and blue from copper ores, turquoise from turquoise, and black and white respectively from shale and gypsum, or from white clays. Usually they were further decorated with feathers of brilliant hues, and sometimes with beads.

Once completed, the prayer stick received its spiritual life and powers in a brief, simple ceremony. Its makers breathed on it, prayed over it, sprinkled it with meal or pollen, waved it in the smoke of a fire. Finally it was placed where its power was needed. It might be kept permanently in the home, or placed by a spring or by the shore of the river, or stored away with food to help preserve it through the winter, or carried in ceremonies, or buried in the ground with the dead. The people knew, of course, that a stick had no virtue beyond that of the prayer that went into it.

Prayer was sometimes very private, very personal, and at other times very public. Public prayers were conducted and supervised by the priests. Each winter just before the solstice, for example, the priests, after prayer and fasting, would petition the sun to begin his long journey back to the zenith. The sun invariably cooperated.

And then there was the dancing, the river people's most characteristic form of public prayer. There were corn dances, rain dances, war dances, all sorts of dances, and in each the prayers, the dance steps, the drumming, the costumes were rigorously prescribed. The prescriptions were quite rigorously followed, too; the priests saw to that.

The various sodalities were the custodians of the rubrics, or rules, for the various dances. They memorized the choruses, complete with drum accompaniment, so that they could lead and guide the people in the particular dance, for every dance had to be performed strictly according to its liturgy. They engaged in or watched over the making of the sacred costumes of skins from the bison of the plains, from the deer of the forest, from the lynx and the fox and the rabbit; of feathers from the brilliant parrots of lands to the south, from their own domesticated turkeys, from eagles and owls; of boughs of evergreen needles from the mountain pines; of corn husks from their fields. Gourds were filled with pebbles, for use as rattles with which to accompany the drums.

There were rehearsals, for a dance might last for many hours and, if performed sloppily, could border on sacrilege, offending rather than pleasing the spirits to whom the prayer was addressed. The women danced daintily on bare feet, while the men, wearing deerskin sandals, pounded the earth with virile persistency. The goal was to perform the entire dance in perfect harmony, for the spirits frowned upon discord in ceremony as in life.

The people—especially the members of the particular sodality—also prepared for each dance with ascetic practices, which were considered spiritually cleansing. They fasted, eating only prescribed foods. They cleaned their homes, removing all refuse to the trash heap outside the village. They swept the central plaza clean, as well as every other place where the dancing might be done. When the day of the dance arrived, everyone was ready for it, ready to participate in it or simply to watch it. Those who merely watched sat on the roofs of their apartments or on the ground along the edge of the plaza. The rising sun etched the village and its shadows in sharp relief. The dawn silently spread its glowing warmth, and all was quiet. Then, suddenly, the drummers began their insistent beat, and the dance began.

The first dancers came leaping, almost flying, out of the hole in the roof of the kiva. A song could be heard blending with the drums, and soon the chorus appeared around a corner and took their positions near the drums. Then around other corners came the main body of dancers in separate groups, joining in the plaza and dancing across the plaza in a kind of quarter-step, shuffling march. The man leading them carried a long, slim pole, at the top of which eagle feathers seemed to mingle with the clouds they resembled. Back and forth across the plaza people danced, back and forth, back and forth. With them, and around them danced the masked kachinas, the demigods of nature's spirit world.

With their gourd rattles, the men imitated the soft rustle of seeds sown by the wind and the patter of rain falling on the thirsty earth. With their eagle feathers, both the men and the women entreated the clouds to release life-giving moisture. With sprigs of evergreen, they prayed for long and healthy lives. And while they did all this, the koshare, the dancing clowns, their naked bodies painted white with black stripes, flitted about the plaza, mimicking the dancers and making fun of them, and generally ridiculing the whole elaborate, solemn ceremony of which they were, nevertheless, a traditional part.

And so the dancing went on, and the fun, too, throughout the day. After the sun had disappeared once again into the underworld, the ceremony ended, the men returning to the kiva, the women and the spectators returning home. The village was quiet again, amid the soft, comforting sounds of satisfied nature.

Such was one element of worship in the religion of the river people. About the element of morals less is known. There was no list of moral precepts such as is found in the world's major religions, yet the people lived by a code of conduct based on a kind of love very similar to that recommended in the New Testament. As suggested earlier, acts of violence against another's person or property were severely condemned. The notion of seeking the welfare not only of loved ones, but of all others in the community as well, seems to have been deeply ingrained in their traditions. They cared affectionate-

The arrival of the Shalako

ly for the very old and the very young, arranging for them to care for each other, and including them in the life of the community. Their humor could be crude and offensive, as was often the case with the koshare in the dances, but their attitude toward the mysteries of sex and procreation was one of respect, even awe, and their dedication to monogamy was admirable. Above all, they were a peaceful people, quietly engaged in the pursuit of as much life, liberty, and happiness as their uncooperative environment and occasional predatory visitors would permit.

▼▲▼▲▼

In the early part of the fifteenth century, disturbing rumors began to drift up from the south. Traders brought reports of pale men dressed in hard, gleaming metal, and riding on the broad backs of great, sleek animals, larger, more powerful, and swifter than the buffalo of the open plains. There were stories that these were gods of the ancient people bent on punishment for transgressions; at least, this was the way that the newcomers, astride their dragons, and armed with terrifying thundersticks, seemed to be conducting themselves. Before long, stories brought word that they were coming closer. The river people waited, in disbelief and trepidation. There was nothing else for them to do.

CHAPTER TWO
SPANISH CONQUEST AND PUEBLO RESISTANCE

*These people indeed would be the most blessed
on earth if they worshipped the true God.*
BARTOLOMÉ DE LAS CASAS
(MID–SIXTEENTH CENTURY)

CURIOUSLY, the first contact the Pueblos of the Rio Grande had with Spaniards was with a Moor named Esteban, or Estevanico, in 1528. He was the slave of Andres Dorantes, a Spanish nobleman and fortune hunter, who had come to the newly discovered continent in search of riches and immortality. The expedition was ill advised and unsuccessful. Instead of gold, the fortune hunters found themselves beset by heat, humidity, endless swamps, and Native Americans in a thoroughly unfriendly mood, for these were not the first Europeans to invade Florida.

After a brief, unpleasant stay, the adventurers beat a rueful retreat to their five frail rawhide boats, headed back for Mexico, and promptly ran into a storm that sank four of the boats and drove the fifth aground in what today is Galveston Bay. Four men ultimately survived, including Esteban and his master. During the next eight years, they walked back to Mexico City over a trackless, erratic route a couple of thousand miles long. Their treatment by Native Americans along the way ranged from enslavement to being revered as powerful medicine men.

Back in Mexico City the wanderers had some tall tales to tell. They described having seen great towns, rich enough to make a natural plunderer's mouth water. The tales naturally grew taller with repeated telling; Esteban was particularly good at embroidery. Intelligent, imaginative, and articulate, he impressed Viceroy Mendoza enough to be bought by him from his master and enlisted as a guide and envoy on a reconnaissance trip to the North, to the so-called Cities of Cibola.

And so it was that Esteban, in March 1539, found himself in the vanguard of a new expedition to the North—this time to obtain information about the geography, topography, natural resources, and inhabitants of the region; to Christianize the natives; and then to claim the land in the name of the Spanish king. The expedition party included Esteban, two Franciscan friars, and some Pima Indians. One of the friars shortly took ill and returned to the Mexican frontier province of Nueva Galicia, leaving Fray Marcos de Niza in charge.

Marcos sent Esteban on ahead with a small advance party. He was to scout for the Seven Cities of Gold and send back runners with reports of their findings in the form of crosses. If the towns he encountered were poor and unremarkable, he was to send back a small cross, five or six inches long. A cross a foot long would indicate a sizable town and plentiful booty.

For reasons lost to history, Esteban's first messenger to Fray Marcos carried a cross five feet long. A month or so later—and after the friar had come across several equally large crosses left behind for him along the way—a second messenger brought news that Esteban was dead. By his account, Esteban's party had reached the Zuni Pueblo of Hawikuh in central New Mexico, where Esteban had been killed.

The incurably optimistic Fray Marcos promptly translated the news about the Zuni Pueblo as new, undiscovered lands rivaling, if not surpassing, Mexico and Peru. One story—his own, and unsupported—proposed that he continued north far enough to take a very cautious peek at the Zuni village from a distant hill. In any case, he decided that it was his duty not to emulate Esteban but rather to return to Mexico and report to the viceroy. First, however, he planted a cross in the vast semidesert region, claiming the land for Spain, and then retreated south for Culiacan, Mexico.

On the strength of Marcos's glowing but undocumented report of the Zuni village, Viceroy Mendoza announced the discovery of Cibola and his plans to send an expedition to conquer it. To command the expedition, the viceroy appointed the ambitious thirty-year-old aristocrat Don Francisco Vasquez de Coronado, the first conquistador ever to venture north of the 30th parallel. He and some of his friars—plus 300 soldiers, a thousand Indian servants, and 1,500 cattle, mules and horses—set out on the long march from Culiacan to Hawikuh. The inhabitants were waiting for them when they finally arrived in early July 1540, for scouts had informed the Pueblo of Coronado's progress from the time they had entered Indian country. From the height of the Zuni Pueblo walls, the Spanish forces must have looked like a great black serpent coming to devour them. They patiently waited until an advance party came within range of the Pueblo and then met them with a discharge of arrows.

Coronado was irritated but not detered by the Zunis' treatment of his emissaries. Though reluctant to spill blood at the gateway to the fabled land of treasure, yet not about to be turned back by the first show of resistance, he and his troop attacked the village.

The Zunis were by no means totally unprepared. They had evacuated the town of all but warriors: the women and children, and nearly all the men under twenty and over sixty had been moved to caves and other places of safety amid some nearby cliffs. They also had taken their portable things to hiding places nearby. Thus the town was occupied only by a few of the elders and the fighting men, the ranks of the latter having been swollen by many warriors from other villages in the area, for evidently there was a widespread feeling that this first encounter with these formidable visitors was crucial.

As the Spaniards approached the village, a thin line of

Don Francisco Vasquez de
Coronado's expedition into
Pueblo Country,
1540–1542

1. Pueblos in Sonora
2. Hopi
3. Zuni
4. Taos Pueblo
5. Pecos Pueblo

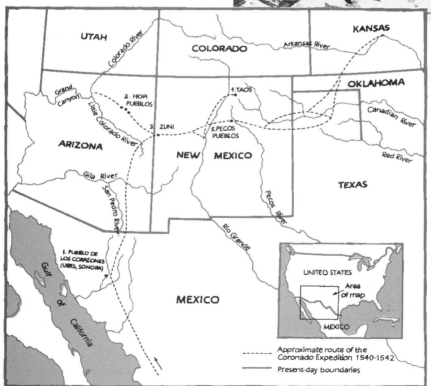

Approximate route of the
Coronado Expedition 1540-1542

Present-day boundaries

Pueblo warriors just outside it tried to warn them back with loud hollering and flailing gestures. When this failed to panic the determined Spaniards into a retreat, the Pueblos became bolder, running out several at a time in brief sallies and discharging arrows at targets of opportunity. Instead of intimidating the attackers, however, this unfriendliness enraged them. After getting Fray Marcos's blessing, Coronado ordered a charge.

The Pueblos immediately dispersed in all directions, many of them back into the village. Despite their hasty withdrawal, the Spaniards managed to kill a dozen or so. To stiffen the attackers' resolve, Fray Marcos worked his way impatiently up from the rear and exhorted the Spaniards to stop shilly-shallying and take the town. Although the invaders were thrown back twice during the skirmish and Coronado was put out of action with an arrow wound in the foot, the Zuni village fell within an hour. Realizing that they could not turn away the Spaniards, the Pueblos had stopped fighting and had asked for a truce. The Spaniards offered to let the Zunis remain in their village, but most wanted to return to the loved ones they had hidden away. They left the invaders in the abandoned village, the latter already gorging themselves on corn and beans and turkey, seasoned with the whitest salt they had ever seen.

If there was food in abundance, the same could not be said for the gold and silver, which Fray Marcos had so vividly predicted would be there. Because of his imaginative and inaccurate stories of Cibola, Marcos became a target of ridicule. Within a few days, he returned in shame to Mexico. Shortly thereafter, Coronado notified Viceroy Mendoza that Fray Marcos had "not told the truth in a single thing that he said, but everything is the opposite of what he related, except the name of the cities and the large stone houses." What did impress the Spaniards about Pueblo culture, however, was their agricultural expertise, their architectural skills, and their successful method of governing.

As the main column of the Spanish army made its way to Hawikuh, Coronado sent out a scouting party to investigate other villages. Led by a Captain Pedro de Tovar, this contingent reached a Hopi village in northeastern Arizona and conquered it very much as the Zuni village had been conquered, even to the detail of being spurred to an attack by one of the friars. They did not occupy it, however, for Tovar was anxious to return to Coronado with a report, particularly including information on a large river which, the Hopis said, flowed through a great crack in the earth located west of their homelands.

The report stirred Coronado's interest. He had been expecting supplies from Mexico for some time, and news of the river raised his hopes that they might be coming by water. Out went another scouting party, this one led by Captain García López de Cárdenas. It found the Colorado River, but at its most inaccessible spot. The crack in the earth turned out to be the Grand Canyon, and the Cárdenas party never got within a thousand feet of the river itself, despite several valiant attempts. Awed by the canyon's immensity and beauty, but crestfallen over the river's inaccessibility, they returned to make their unhappy report.

Meanwhile, Coronado was visited by representatives from Cicuye, a large pueblo to the east approximately 200 miles away, near the Pecos River. In the friendly delegation were two headmen. Because Coronado could not pronounce the names they had given him, he called one Bigotes ("Mustache") and the other Cacique ("Governor"). Although they could not satisfactorily answer Coronado's questions about the location of gold and silver, the visitors assured him that the land to the east was rich in many other ways. They presented him with gifts of hides and spoke to him of the abundant herds of buffalo that roamed the prairies to the east. With his interest piqued, Coronado dispatched Captain Hernando de Alvarado and a small scouting party to the east, ordering them to make all natives subjects of the Spanish Empire and also to keep a lookout for the famous treasure that must exist somewhere.

Guided by Bigotes and Cacique, the little band of explorers left Hawikuh. Their first stop was at the village of Acoma, approximately seventy miles away. Atop a high mesa, it was, one of the party reported later, the strongest natural fortress in the world, so high that only the best of muskets could loft a ball to the top. Alvarado and some of his men managed to scrabble their way up to the town, where they exchanged gifts and chatted briefly with the inhabitants—awkwardly and mostly in sign language.

From Acoma the party traveled east until they reached the Rio Grande valley. Here they turned north, following the river to a point some fifteen miles north of modern Albuquerque, where they set up camp near a large village on the west bank, in the heart of Pueblo territory. The invaders' reputation for military might, based chiefly on the size of their stupendous steeds and the lethal power of their magic thundersticks, obviously had prepared the natives along their route to opt for discretion before valor. When Alvarado sent Bigotes into the village with a cross and a promise that the visitors had come in peace, the villagers responded with a promise that they would be received in friendly fashion and supplied with whatever they needed for continuing their journey.

They were as good as their word. On the next day hundreds of them from the twelve villages in the area surrounded the newcomers, offering them food, cotton cloth, and animal skins. They did not issue an invitation to room and board; probably, having learned how little the Zunis had gained by resistance, they had decided that the only way to avoid partial or total eviction by these tourists would be to somehow encourage them on their way. There were, they assured Alvarado, more than fifty other villages to the north, along the river, which he surely would want to see.

Alvarado continued his journey north to Tiguex, the name the Spaniards gave to a group of twelve Pueblo villages they considered a province. After spending several days in the bountiful environment, Alvarado sent word to Coronado that Tiguex would make good winter headquarters for the entire Spanish expedition. On receiving this message several days later, Coronado was delighted and immediately began making preparations for the move.

Meanwhile, Alvarado's group made its way up the Rio Grande, with similarly friendly "pass-them-along" treatment

Antonio de Mendoza (A) was Viceroy of Mexico when Coronado carried out his orders to make all natives subjects of the Spanish Empire. Coronado's first stop was at the village of Acoma (B), a strong natural fortress.

at the many villages along the way—San Ildefonso, Tesuque, Santa Clara, and San Juan. Taos pueblo was perhaps the busiest trading center, situated as it was at the northern border of their territory. Second to it in this respect was Pecos, at the eastern border, to which Bigotes and Cacique led the party of treasure hunters.

Pecos was an impressive town, a strong fortress that had long withstood the persistent raids of the nomadic hunters of the plains. In these battles, slaves were taken occasionally on both sides. Alvarado and company spent some time at Pecos, investigating the edges of the vast plains to the east and marveling at the almost equally vast herds of wandering buffalo. During his stay, Alvarado got to know two slaves from Quivira—one called Turk and the other Ysopete. Turk told him that Quivira was a golden land of untold wealth, far more than enough to fulfill the Spaniards' wildest dreams. Bigotes and Cacique knew of this, he added, for when he was captured by the people of Pecos, they took the golden bracelet he was wearing.

The mention of a golden bracelet was enough to dissipate any further curiosity Alvarado may have had about buffalo. He returned to Pecos forthwith and demanded that Bigotes and Cacique relinquish the gold bracelet. When they flatly denied any knowledge of it, Alvarado ordered them to be manacled, informing the villagers that he would take them back with him, together with Turk and Ysopete, for a proper inquisition by Coronado himself. The villagers, as yet unaccustomed to such conduct, were shocked by this announcement, charging him with bad faith and with repaying kindness with injury. They even started a fight to rescue the prisoners, but superior European arms prevailed. At this point Turk upset Alvarado's plans by inconsiderately escaping.

Alvarado responded to the news of the escape by threatening to stay at Pecos, with his two former guides in irons, until Turk was caught and brought back. Since he had already long overstayed his welcome, this threat was enough to prompt Bigotes to offer to lead a pursuit party, with Cacique to remain a prisoner until Turk was returned. Alvarado reluctantly agreed, and Turk was soon caught and brought back. Immediately, Alvarado's solider band, with the four hapless prisoners literally in chains, marched off to the Rio Grande.

Meanwhile, Captain Cárdenas had arrived with an advance party to set up winter accommodations near the Rio Grande for Coronado's entire travel party. It was now late autumn. The days were getting chilly, especially the mornings, and the nights were becoming intolerably cold. Since the winter nights ahead promised acute discomfort for any open-air campers, Coronado persuaded the inhabitants of Tiquex to move out. There was plenty of room outside the village, where they would find things less crowded during the several months ahead. (The ruins of the village still stand on a low bluff overlooking the Rio Grande near the modern town of Bernalillo. They are called, most appropriately, the Coronado State Monument.)

Upon Coronado's arrival at the Rio Grande, an interview with Turk was a high priority. After his experience with Fray Marcos's imaginative tall tales, Coronado might have been expected to show some trace of skepticism, but the more Turk's tales about Quivira grew—a river five miles wide, containing "fish as big as horses," and numberless kingdoms filled with gold—the larger grew the Great Commander's hope chest. Immediately, he called for Bigotes and Cacique to be interrogated again about the gold bracelet—this time tortured until they confessed. But no amount of pain would extract a confession from the two recalcitrants, and Coronado had to put the matter on hold. He turned his attention, instead, to more- pressing problems such as lack of food and supplies and the approaching winter. He and his advance party decided to settle down, wait for the arrival of the main invasion force (still trudging riverward from the west), and then all make themselves at home at Tiguex for the winter.

To the other eleven villages of Tiguex, Coronado sent agents, accompanied by soldiers, to ask for large but specific amounts of food and clothing to help get his people through the coming winter. As a gentlemen devoted to the amenities of civilized behavior, he instructed the agents to make their requests courteously. He manifestly neglected, however, to instruct them on how to proceed if any of the villagers should refuse this requisition. And nearly all the villagers did refuse, partly because the agents neglected to engage in the customary group discussion and the decision-making process that was an integral part of Pueblo ritual in such events. The Spanish agents and their fellow foragers, having received no instruction on how to deal with refusal, simply took what they wanted from the less agile villagers, in some cases reaching down from their horses and yanking robes and blankets from the wearers' backs. This disrespectful behavior and cultural clash brought about a variety of ill will on both sides and had lasting effects.

In any event, the new residents of Tiguex were pretty well supplied now, although the imminent arrival of the main army might be expected to generate a new round of requests. The possibility of another round, which could utterly devastate them, provided the final thrust to galvanize the resentful Pueblo into organizing meetings among leaders representing several towns to discuss resistance against further use of their communities as free sources of food and clothing. By this time their image of the horse had quieted down considerably from their first impression of a man-eating dragon, and they decided that depriving the soldiers of their transportation might do something toward equalizing the discouraging military imbalance.

One morning, not long after the acquisitive courtesy calls, the Spaniards were alarmed to see a Mexican who had been guarding their horses stagger into their newly acquired village with blood on his clothing and shock in his eyes. The natives had attacked the lightly guarded corral. One of the guards had been killed, the others had discreetly retired, and the rebellious Pueblo were herding the horses back to their villages. Coronado immediately directed Captain Cárdenas to take a party of men and investigate. The captain assembled his group at once and started off after the rebels. After rounding up stray horses, Cárdenas passed a village about five miles north of Tiguex that was holding a large number of horses. He entered with the hope of retrieving the horses and managed to get some of the guards into a sign-language conversation. But the people were uncooperative and defiant. Knowing his small party was outnumbered a hundred to one, Cárdenas turned and led his horse herders back to Tiguex.

Cárdenas's report was not acceptable to Coronado, who evidently couldn't believe that the Pueblo people could be exhibiting such hostility toward them. He ordered Cárdenas to return to the defiant village and retrieve the horses. Cárdenas obediently returned, finding the Pueblos more recalcitrant than before. Back he went with the unbelievable news to Coronado, who thereupon called a council of war.

It was brief. The captains' consensus was clear: these upstarts would have to be dealt with, decisively and promptly, before their aberration became epidemic. The friars gave their blessing in advance to anything Coronado might do to restore God's law and order in the land. Thus armed with both sword and cross, he dispatched two or three captains.

Coronado was not in the happiest of circumstances for this declaration of war. His main army had not yet arrived. His available troops were heavily outnumbered. But they were by no means outgunned, and he was counting on their superior armor and armament to see him through the crisis. In any case, he felt that he had to squelch this effrontery at once, for it could seriously imperil his essential mission. The rewards would be immeasurable for a soldier who could report to his governor or king that he had conquered lands of unlimited spoils, and for the friar who could report to his superior or his God that he had baptized countless souls.

Evidently the effrontery was merely symptomatic of a bitter resentment spreading up along the river. The news was racing through the land faster than Coronado imagined, news that his arrival on the scene could mean eviction, expropriation, forced submission to unfamiliar gods, mistreatment, torture for the unmanageable, even selection for work as slaves in the Mexican mines. The Pueblo people had known fear before, but never fear such as this. Yet they were determined to resist.

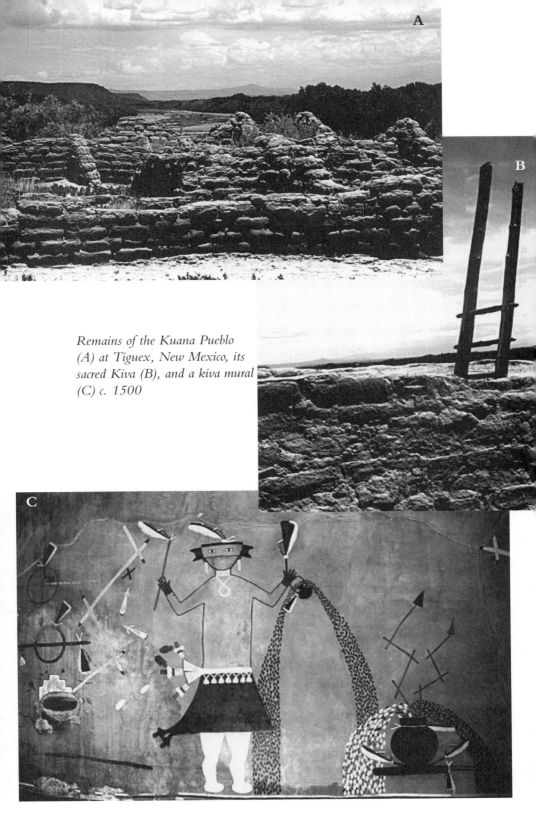

Remains of the Kuana Pueblo (A) at Tiguex, New Mexico, its sacred Kiva (B), and a kiva mural (C) c. 1500

Cárdenas's instructions were to return to the rebellious village with around sixty cavalrymen and some infantry, and again to offer the malcontents their chances for redemption. If they refused, he was to make the offer forcefully enough to persuade them to accept it. He marched to the village with his party and made his offer, but his reception was the same as before. Having thus done his duty, Cárdenas prepared the attack. After arranging his cavalry in a circle around the village to foil any attempts at escape, he gave the Santiago battle cry, and the soldiers began to attack. (The "Santiago!", a prayer to the Spanish patron saint, James, was a conventional effort of the times to enlist the help of heaven in noble enterprises.)

The bloody battle lasted several hours. By evening the attackers had managed to drive the defenders from the roofs and into their apartments. This left the attackers in an unfamiliar situation: they were in command of the village but not of its inhabitants. How long a siege might last under such circumstances no one knew. So the besiegers settled down for the night to consider the problem.

The next morning, Cárdenas again urged the villagers to submit peaceably but was again refused. The battle was resumed. Spaniards were ordered off the roofs, and the cavalrymen again encircled the village. A detachment with a battering ram outside the village made a breach in the lower portion of an outer wall, and heavy smudge fires were set in and near the opening. The smoke poured into the apartments and spread rapidly from room to room, driving the choking residents out through the holes in the roofs and then off the roofs to the ground, where many were killed or captured. Some of the captured were hauled away and pent up in a tent just outside the village. Others—about 200, all told—were dragged out of the village, manacled to stakes, and burned to death in conformance with the customary treatment of heretics and saints and other nonconformists in Europe. Coronado made Bigotes, Cacique, Turk, and Ysopete witness the treatment of the captured.

It was a devastating victory. In its own small way it reflected the experience of earlier gutsy Spaniards in the Americas, as in the victories of Pizarro's and Cortés's tiny bands against seemingly endless odds. Only a few villagers had escaped holocaust, but enough to spread the word along the river of the newcomers' courage in battle, their power and cunning, and their treatment of the defeated. According to records, most of the villagers had surrendered because of a promise of freedom, that some of the Spanish leaders had made to them but neglected to mention to Cárdenas. Whether Cárdenas knew about the truce before giving orders to burn the pueblo is not clear. Whatever the explanation, this aspect of the disaster further weakened the Pueblo's belief in the words of Spanish officers and gentlemen.

It was now the latter part of December 1540. Cold and snow had settled in the valley. Coronado's advance party had been joined by the main army, but his military troubles were not over yet: he had won a battle but not necessarily the war. Instinctively turning to Cárdenas again, he ordered the tough captain to pay a call on each of the eleven villages along the northern part of the river and to subdue them, peacefully or otherwise. This proved to be a rather brief assignment, for Cárdenas found every village deserted: the inhabitants had simply evacuated to the two northernmost villages, where they believed they would be as far away as possible from the invaders without leaving their territory altogether. This evacuation, carried out in unusually severe winter weather, must have been a difficult and terribly uncomfortable thing to do, and it further resulted in much of the population of many villages being crowded into two. The operation suggests something, surely, about the intensity of the people's motivation.

Of the two villages, one called Moho was reportedly the hotbed of resistance, led by a man whom the Spaniards were to call Juan Alemán. (One of the innovations of baptism, the river people were discovering, was that it deprived them of the names they had always lived with, substituting strange and meaningless sounds.) Coronado chose captain Maldenado to take a small detachment to Moho and inform Alemán that the people would be pardoned for their sins of rebellion if they surrendered and would be severely punished if they did not. The villagers, however, seemed unable to grasp the notion that resisting invaders constituted rebellion. They had yet to achieve a satisfactory appreciation of the moral authority so conspicuously displayed by the newcomers. Indeed, they now were especially reluctant to take their word for anything. And so the captain's party, unable to coax the Pueblos into submission, and too weak to compel them, returned and made their report.

Coronado enlisted Cárdenas once again as head of a second band of soldiers, marching north to subdue the hostiles. At some small distance from Moho, after halting the detachment, he approached the warrior-studded walls with three horsemen and, calling out and making signs, repeated Coronado's standard offer. From one of the roofs Alemán replied with friendly words and signs of welcome and suggested that he and the captain, both unarmed and unattended, meet near the entrance to the village and embrace in token of their friendship. Cárdenas agreed, unfortunately underestimating the effect that Spanish example had had on the Pueblos. Alemán's embrace was enthusiastically tight, pinning the captain's arms to his sides and giving several Pueblos concealed nearby an opportunity to attack him. Not even Cárdenas's helmeted head could have withstood the blows of the hatchets he received. The Pueblos lifted the limp Cárdenas over their heads and proceeded to carry him into the village. Only stunned by the hatchet blows, Cárdenas recovered in a few minutes and prevented his bearers from squeezing him through the narrow opening of the village walls. Despite a rain of arrows and stones from the roof, his bodyguard and a few other soldiers rescued him. Several were injured in the fracas, including the tough captain himself. Although Cárdenas was wounded in the leg by an arrow, he was by no means put out of action. That he was taken by surprise, however, had a profound effect on him, and he decided to leave Moho under guard and try his luck with another rebellious village.

There, his luck was no better, athough he was discreet enough to avoid giving anyone an opportunity for another personal attack. The resisters' loud and ribald yells and signs, followed by flights of arrows, were formidable enough to persuade Cárdenas to return to Moho, where he was welcomed this time by hit-and-run attacks.

Now it was Cárdenas's turn to try some trickery. Pretending to retreat, his party lured some of the bolder Pueblo fighters out onto the plain and then wheeled around and attacked them, felling quite a few of their leaders. But since this was a one-time tactic, and the situation looked as difficult as the one he had met with at the previous village, Cárdenas decided to return to headquarters, in the hope of convincing Coronado to bring all his forces to bear on the stubborn problem.

If that was his hope, it was not in vain. Within a few days, the entire army appeared before Moho, ominously equipped with scaling ladders. Again they gave the standard offer, and again they faced rejection with derisive shouts and signs. So the army encircled the town, Coronado sounded the "Santiago" cry, and the battle was on. The attackers tried first to breach the outer wall but found that beneath its surface coat was a foundation of trees planted solidly in the ground, with tough willow laths woven through them. To their astonishment, it was impregnable. Next they tried scaling the walls, and after many setbacks did reach the first tier of roofs, but here they discovered that the defenders had cunningly knocked out the roofs of the rooms in front of the second tier, leaving the climbers with nothing on which to rest their ladders for their assault on that tier. Meanwhile the Spaniards were bombarded by endless flights of arrows from above, many with poisoned tips. Little of this resistance was fatal to the well-armored Spaniards—only a half dozen or so died in, or immediately after, the battle—but it was effective in turning them away.

Coronado's attempt to seize the village by storm had failed, so he relied on another tactic to weaken the village and make it susceptible to attack. Recognizing that the village was doubtless well supplied with food but hoping that it might be short of water, he waited for the opportune time to reattempt a siege. The well the villagers had dug caved in on the diggers, burying some two dozen of them, and their prospects for water seemed bleak. But the winter, which had been so unusually cruel, came to their rescue in the form of a long and heavy snowfall, which continued intermittently for several weeks and gave them at least enough water to get by on.

Meanwhile, the besiegers, buffeted by the biting cold of the nights and muddy dampness of the days, huddled in their miserable tent city, planned another assault. They made elaborate battering rams and even cannon out of timbers but couldn't get them to work. The days dragged on into March. Soon the Moho defenders were once again without water. By around the middle of March they were so desperate that they requested a parley. An agreement was reached, a period of armistice was arranged, and the pathetic transfer took place.

During these negotiations, Coronado offered a guarantee of amnesty if the villagers would surrender to cross and crown. They declined the honor, explaining frankly that none of them had any faith in such a guarantee; they were desperate, obviously, but not that desperate.

Meanwhile the Spaniards were themselves becoming a bit desperate. The nights were still cold, the days not exactly sultry, and many of the soldiers were suffering from exposure. Coronado sent Cárdenas to Zia, a village northwest of Moho to get food and clothing. Reluctant to use unnecessary force—his experience at Moho seems to have increased his respect for native resistance—he merely asked for clothing and was astonished by the friendly response. Despite their own cold-weather needs, the people of Zia gave him a considerable amount of supplies—enough to relieve much of the suffering back at tent city. Their response may have been due to fear, leading them to choose the less desirable of two alternatives. It may have been due to ignorance, for the regional broadcasting system, though active and widespread, was by no means infallible. Or it may have been due to something else, at least partly, that the people of Zia and Moho were not the most stalwart of friends.

The people of Moho, in any case, had no friends who

could bring them water, and now thirst was about to defeat these doughty defenders who had withstood the full military might of the aggressors. But rather than die of thirst, they decided to make a run for it. With the remaining women and children interspersed among the warriors for protection, the people of Moho stole away one night near the end of March. A Spaniard happened to see them, however, and gave the alarm. In the ensuing pandemonium, most were killed or captured, some were wounded and froze to death during the night, some were drowned in the river, and a few escaped.

The long show of resistance was over. Moho was put to the torch, with Bigotes and his three fellow prisoners again forced to watch. The smaller village to the north was soon subdued by a combination of siege and assault, with some of its people scattered but most either killed or captured and enslaved. Along the river there settled an empty silence of utter devastation, broken only by the beat of horses hooves, the shouts and calls of soldiers, and the creaking and clanking of bloody arms and armor, glorious in victory.

On or about April Fool's Day, Coronado turned his attention to Turk's tall tales again. Quivira, growing more golden with every new detail, beckoned irresistibly. Yet the commander felt that he couldn't start east quite yet. The events that had culminated with the sack of Moho had for some reason alienated most, if not all, Pueblos living on both sides of the river. As a result, he was very hesitant about leaving such hostility behind to fester and perhaps interfere with his return trip from Quivira, when his troops presumably would be both burdened and preoccupied with weighty treasure. One of his captains suggested that an advance party be sent to find Quivira and report back, but Coronado would have none of it. He believed that if the ruler of Quivira were only half as powerful as Turk had described him, he would be the equivalent of half a dozen Montezumas and should be approached only by the entire expeditionary army.

So an image-repairing campaign was undertaken among the Pueblos show them what gentle, harmless, peace-loving people the Spaniards really were. As a gesture of friendship, Coronado returned Cacique to Pecos. He kept Bigotes hostage but promised that he too would be returned on the way to Quivira if the Pueblos did not cause trouble. After about three weeks of sending olive-branch emissaries hither and yon, the commander decided that the Pueblos seemed sufficiently tranquilized for him to get started for the land of opportunity.

The journey began on April 23, 1541, with provisions for thirty days. Merely gathering these provisions must have been no small undertaking. According to Castañeda, whose figures may be somewhat inflated, the expeditionary force was back to full strength: some fifteen hundred people with a thousand horses, half that many cattle, and five times that many sheep! One can imagine the noise that must have accompanied its slow progress over hill and dale and plain. One can well imagine also the relief that Bigotes must have felt when, as the expedition plodded past the village of Pecos, Coronado kept his promise and released him. There must have been considerable relief among the villagers, too, as they realized that the Spaniards were only passing by on their way to the land of the buffalo.

The expedition traveled southeast in search of a good place to cross the Pecos River, swollen by the melting of the winter's heavy snows. At the site of present-day Anton Chico, a bridge had to be built, and the crossing was achieved without casualties or other misfortunes. Continuing east, with the Rio Grande Pueblos behind them, the adventurers came upon the Canadian River and followed its eastward course, approaching what is now the Texas Panhandle. Here, Coronado wrote later, he entered upon plains so vast that he never reached their end, although he traveled over them for almost a thousand miles. The buffalo were without number, and not a day went by during his entire journey on the plains when the buffalo weren't visible.

On the plains the soldiers noticed long marks that might have been made by the dragging of spears. Following these marks, the expedition came across bands of natives much different from those they had previously met. They were

One of the earliest known engravings of a buffalo,
found in a French publication in 1558.

nomadic buffalo hunters, and the marks had been made by
dragging long poles for their tents. But the dragging, interestingly enough, was done not by the people but by their
dogs. Indeed, in the lives of these nomads, the explorers discovered, there were only two animals of any real importance:
the buffalo and the dog. The people followed the buffalo and
were followed by the dogs.

From the buffalo they obtained food, clothing, and shelter, and—indirectly through trade with the Rio Grande people—some corn, cotton cloth, and pottery. They ate buffalo
meat, lightly roasted or raw, and drank the blood while it was
still warm. They also cut buffalo meat into strips, dried the
strips in the sun, and then ground them into a mash which
they stored; this was, essentially, the food called pemmican that
northern tribes generally used as a kind of high-protein hard-
tack. The buffalo hunters peeled the skin off their prey skill-

fully with their flint knives, tanning the hides expertly for their tents, their outer clothing, and their footwear; and from the beasts' hairy shoulders they even obtained wool. They used the sinews for tough thread, the bones for awls, the bladders for jugs, and the dung for fuel. Clearly, there wasn't much left of a buffalo when they were finished with it.

Like the Eskimo, they used their dogs as beasts of burden, even providing them with pack saddles, which were cinched with straps of buffalo leather. The dogs followed them as they moved about the plains, carrying the tenting hides and dragging the poles behind them. The loads, Castañeda estimated, ranged between thirty and fifty pounds, depending on the size of the dog.

Coronado, still under the Turk's spell, had sent the Quiviran ahead to parley with the buffalo hunters. When he returned, he had a new story to tell. The land of treasure, he said, was not to the northeast as many believed, but to the east. Coronado disregarded the growing distrust of Turk and frequent and fervent protests of Ysopete, who insisted that Quivira was neither an eastern land nor a rich one, and led his roving horde straight east as far as the Palo Duro canyon, now a state park in the Texas Panhandle southeast of Amarillo. What Turk was up to no one knew, but Castañeda's account of the vast, featureless plains over which they crossed (covered by a buffalo grass so tough, he wrote, that the expedition left no trail behind it) suggests there must have been strong suspicions that the imaginative guide hoped to get the tourists so thoroughly lost and confused that he might escape before they found out, if they ever did, what a wild-goose chase they were engaged in.

At Palo Duro, Coronado came to his senses, deciding finally that the only thing he seemed to be heading for was the rising sun. He put Turk in chains, and made Ysopete number one guide, to lead him and a small force north while the main expeditionary force found its way as best it could back to headquarters on the Rio Grande. Roaming deep into present-day Kansas, Coronado's party found nothing rich but the soil. Utterly frustrated, the commander acceded to a popular demand that the truth be extracted from Turk by torture. The inquiry was successful. Turk confessed that, at the insistence of the people at Pecos and on the plains, he was to lead the invaders so far out on the plains that they would become permanently lost or so weakened by their wanderings and the loss of horses and supplies that they would die, or fail to resist attack by the people when they tried to return. Enraged by this confession, the Spaniards killed Turk. Then the despondent adventurers headed back for the Rio Grande.

The Pueblos had been awaiting their return. Their anxiety, however, proved to be generally unfounded, for the returnees were far too tired and discouraged to create the kind of havoc that had characterized their earlier visitation. Arriving back at their headquarters in mid-September 1541, the explorers settled down for a winter of planning their next move. Some, including Coronado, wanted to take another crack at Quivira in the spring. Others wanted to give up the whole enterprise and return to the relative safety and comfort of Mexico. And still others didn't know what they wanted to do.

Their decision was taken out of their hands late in December. Coronado, while out riding with Captain Maldenado, fell from his horse when a saddle strap broke. As he fell, he was struck on the head by a horse's hoof. From that time on, he was a changed man. Ill, depressed, irritable, and gloomy, Coronado soon determined that the expedition was finally over. And so, in the spring, the invaders departed, leaving behind an experience from which the river people would never fully recover.

Gradually, as they became convinced that they were not likely to see their visitors again, they returned to the more tranquil life they had known. The villages in the Moho region slowly came back to life. The fields were cultivated again, and the harmony of life was restored. As the years passed, and as the elders died and the young replaced them, memories of the nightmare grew dimmer but never completely disappeared.

For almost forty years the river people lived in a state of blissful neglect. Then one day in the late summer of 1581 a group of twenty-eight Spaniards (three friars, nine soldiers, and sixteen Mexican servants) appeared at Puaray, a village not far from Coronado's old headquarters in the province of Tiguex. Although the sight must have been rather unsettling, the villagers, reassured by the size of the party, received them courteously if not affectionately. The visit was brief and uneventful. The villagers listened impassively to the friars' arguments for their conversion, arguments which proved too insubstantial to outweigh community memories.

Despite the presence of soldiers, the Pueblos declined the friars' requests for their conversion. The party soon left to explore new territories. First they marched east to Pecos and then retraced their route west, continuing as far as Zuni. At Zuni the soldiers announced that they had decided to return to Mexico. The friars, frustrated by their failure to convert a single soul along their route, protested, and in the ensuing discussion it was agreed that the soldiers would escort them back to Puaray, leaving them there to try their luck again. Such decisions were to be characteristic of the hundreds of evangelical missionaries who would infiltrate the Southwest over the next several centuries, their considerable dedication and courage to be matched only by the impassive sales resistance of an already fervently religious people.

The Puaray villagers could not have been very happy to see the friars so soon again, especially as resident proselytizers. After the soldiers had gone, the friars were at their mercy. Furthermore, the missionaries had some possessions—horses, some goats, and some minor commodities that they had brought along for trading. These unarmed men were undoubtedly harmless, but whether the nervous villagers were convinced of this is quite another matter. Probably the friars at best were considered uninvited nuisances, especially by religious leaders alarmed by the threat of foreign competition. In any case, the villagers' final solution to the problem of the friars was to kill them. Then some measure of peace was restored along the river.

About a year and a half later, in early 1583, another small party arrived, this one comprising only sixteen men: a friar, fourteen soldiers, and a civilian named Antonio de Espejo. Espejo, a prosperous rancher and mine owner in Mexico, was wealthy enough to finance a modest expedition into New Mexico. He had recently concluded that a tour outside Mexico could be beneficial to his health, ever since he was wanted for the murder of a few ranch hands. He located a friar who was interested in venturing north to learn the fate of the two missionaries whom the soldiers had left behind at Puaray and urged him to persuade his superiors to authorize a small expeditionary force for that purpose. Since the rancher had offered to underwrite the cost, the superiors gave their blessing to the enterprise (which was nonetheless illegal, because expeditions into New Mexico could be authorized only by authorities in Madrid, Spain). The arrangement apparently was that Espejo, for all his financial input, would be merely tagging along as a kind of observer. But by the time the party had reached the southernmost group of Rio Grande villages (near Socorro), Espejo had been elected leader.

As the party approached Puaray, the villagers fled, fearful that this might be a visit of vengeful retribution. Although some communication was established, and the Spaniards tried to reassure them that they would not be punished, the villagers refused to return, evidently wishing to protect the guilty individuals from identification and themselves from an inquisition that might be conducted for that purpose. So the visitors, making themselves at home in the village, paused to consider their next move.

The villagers' precautionary evacuation of Puaray was to prove rather typical of the many encounters between well-armed but heavily outnumbered Spanish soldiers and the hundreds of warriors whom they defeated or caused to flee in terror. One immediate explanation for the reaction is that the warriors were chronically chickenhearted, but this is flatly contradicted by the countless references in Spanish records to their impressive bravery in battle, especially against the totally unfamiliar terrors of warhorses, thundersticks, and even cannon. A more likely explanation is the hatred of war among Pueblos, even among the warriors, who normally were

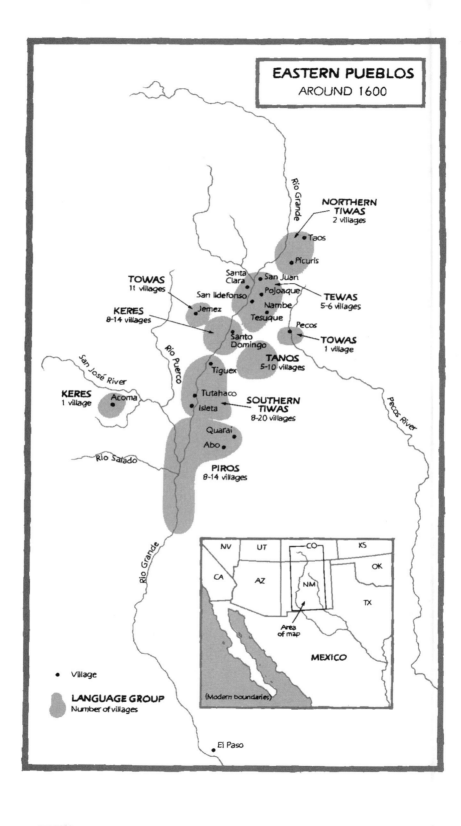

EASTERN PUEBLOS
AROUND 1600

NORTHERN
TIWAS
2 villages

• Taos

• Picuris

Santa
Clara

• San Juan

Pojoaque

San Ildefonso

Nambe

TEWAS
5-6 villages

TOWAS
11 villages

• Jemez

Tesuque

• Pecos

KERES
8-14 villages

Santo
Domingo

TOWAS
1 village

TANOS
5-10 villages

Tiguex

KERES
1 village

Tutahaco

• Acoma

Isleta

SOUTHERN
TIWAS
8-20 villages

Quarai

Abo •

Rio Salado

PIROS
8-14 villages

Rio Grande

Rio Grande

San José River

Rio Puerco

Pecos River

El Paso

• Village

LANGUAGE GROUP
Number of villages

NV   UT   CO   KS

CA   AZ   NM   OK

TX

Area
of map

MEXICO

(Modern boundaries)

defenders rather than aggressors, and for whom war could never be better than a last resort. If the Europeans had come to learn instead of to teach, Europe might have been spared much suffering.

None of the harsh treatment accorded the river people was sanctioned by officially stated policy. The governmental archives, in Madrid and Mexico City, were full of edicts ordering the Spaniards to treat Native Americans with justice and kindness. But these directives lost much of their flavor in translation at the operational level. And none of them directed that the natives simply be let alone.

Having achieved their objective, most of Espejo's little band expected to head for home. Espejo himself, however, was not eager to go back so soon, for obvious reasons. The longer he delayed, the weaker the not-so-long arm of justice was likely to become. Further, the party had found evidence of minerals along their route, and they had been told of potentially rich mines further north. If Espejo could take solidly encouraging reports back to Mexico, what honors he imagined would be in store for him!

With a pious declaration that he now had an opportunity to serve His Majesty by visiting another undiscovered country, he led his band of adventurers to the northeast and visited many villages previously unseen by foreign eyes. Then, turning back west, he paid calls on the sky city, Acoma, and on villages in the Zuni and Hopi territories. Finally, he swung east again to the great river, checking on Taos and other northern settlements. For all its false beginnings, the Espejo expedition turned out to be a genuine feat of exploration, yielding much information about the land and its people. The party visited some six dozen villages, discovering that the people of the Rio Grande and its tributaries, though sharing a common way of life and many similar customs and beliefs, were clearly divided by different language groups. It also became clear that the divisions went deeper than language. An individual's commitment was first to his family, then to his clan, then to his village, and finally to his language group. The recognition of this lack of unity was to serve the foreigners well.

Another remarkable feature of the Espejo expedition was its generally good relations with Native Americans. Throughout most of its travels the expedition was showered with gifts and valuable information about native customs. The party was too small to be very formidable, and the news probably had been spread that it did not seem to be merely an advance group, paving the way for an armed multitude hard on its heels. In addition, so small a party could be rather easily supplied; this man was no Coronado, demanding all of a village's winter stores. Some credit also may be due to Espejo, who, whatever his history, now proved less unpleasant in his dealings with the natives than the gentlemen they had met forty years earlier.

There were two exceptions. The first was minor: an almost ludicrous scrape with the Hopi people. The second was major, and it must have thoroughly restored the reputation which the Coronado expedition had earned throughout New Mexico. On their return to Tiguex, Espejo and his group were met by warriors on the walls of the first village, shouting at them derisively. At Puaray, too, to their astonishment and alarm, they received the same kind of greeting, as well as a flat refusal to provide them with any supplies. In self-defense, the intruders decided that they would have to administer "some punishment" to Pueblos or they would lose control.

The village, they discovered, was deserted, except for about thirty warriors on the roofs. Appointing four men to stand guard at the four corners of the village, Espejo ordered others to set fire to the town, and still others to capture any warriors that tried to escape. Some of the warriors were burned to death; at least, Espejo thought so because of their cries. Others, trying to escape, were captured and imprisoned in one of the kivas. After the fire had died down somewhat and no more cries could be heard, the captured warriors were brought out of the kiva. In a grove of cottonwood trees outside the village, they were lined up and killed.

The expedition now headed east again. At Pecos they found that the news of Puaray's fate had preceded them. A reported 2,000 warriors stood guard over the town. The expedition's request for food was brusquely refused. Since the party needed food badly, however, six soldiers entered the town and took what was needed, as well as capturing a man and a woman to act as guides to the country of the buffalo. Whatever Spanish soldiers may have lacked, it was not courage. Whatever the Pecos warriors may have lacked, it was not self-control.

After following the Pecos River south into western Texas, the explorers switched back west of the Rio Grande, reaching Mexico some ten months after they had left it. Espejo, whose glowing reports evidently saved him from the prosecution he had been trying to avoid, died in 1586, on his way to Madrid to plead for an appointment as captain of a band of colonists.

The idea of colonizing the middle Rio Grande valley had been shuffled about in the suspense files of the Spanish government for about ten years. Colonies along the river would not only establish some degree of certainty over the territory but also provide a permanent base for explorations of the vast areas to the east and west in search of ever receding treasure and the promise of the more fundamental riches of field and farm. The jostling among the contenders for the honor of being His Majesty's pioneer colonizer, however, caused so many paper jams in bureaucratic channels that the necessary authorization was not to be handed down for about another ten years. During that time, there were a few minor incursions into New Mexico, but only one major one worth recounting.

Gaspar Castaño de Sosa was an affluent miner, rancher, and slave trader living in the province of Nuevo Leon, in northern Mexico. Eager to seek fame and fortune by heading a colonial expedition into New Mexico, he twice appealed to Mexico City for permission and was twice refused. He also was ordered to stop his traffic in slaves, irritating him no end. Deciding that the law against entering New Mexico without permission did not apply to provincial officials like himself—for at the time he was the lieutenant governor and military commander of Nuevo Leon—Castaño de Sosa began gathering supplies and recruiting people for the expedition. The people of his home town and its environs were almost all his employees, and he knew that they would jump at a chance to escape from the peonage which, until this moment, he had considered quite suitable. To whet their appetites, he showed them some high-quality silver which, he solemnly assured them, had been found in the country where they would be going.

In August of 1590, Castaño, in the hope of finding undiscovered riches, set out with 170 men, women, and children, as well as a long line of horses, cattle, supply wagons, and even two-wheeled cannons. A retinue of slaves was gradually added by means of irresistible invitations issued along the way. By November, the expedition reached its first objective—the Pecos River. Here it turned north, heading for the village of Pecos.

The news of its progress spread throughout the territory. All along the way, Native Americans could be seen silently observing from a respectful distance, usually from across the river. There was no communication of any significance, nor were there any acts of hostility except at one location where the natives (evidently Apaches) picked off a straggler and stole a few oxen.

By now food stores were alarmingly low, and the explorers were subsisting mainly on a diet of fish from the river and pods from the plentiful mesquite bush. It was early December, and the cold was beginning to bite. Castaño, eager to find a village with which to share his troubles, sent a dozen men ahead to reconnoiter, instructing their leader, a man named Heredia, to try to bring back a native or two for questioning about villages in the vicinity. Under no circumstances, he warned, was the group to enter any village; that should be done only by the expedition as a whole. He had gotten the distinct impression that the natives might not be very friendly.

During the next two weeks he heard from Heredia only twice, when a couple of men from the group returned for supplies. Had they seen any villages? any people? Not a one, they replied, but they were continuing their search. Then, two days before Christmas, the scouting party reappeared looking rather battered. Most of the men had no weapons, some had no horses, and several of those with horses were riding bareback. Heredia reported with some embarrassment that they had disobeyed their orders.

The first settlement they had come across turned out to be Pecos. The cold and snow had compelled them to enter it. The villagers had proved quite friendly, feeding them, giving them a supply of corn, and even putting them up for the night. But the next morning, when Heredia asked for more supplies to take back to the main expedition, warriors attacked his party without warning. Falling back to their rooms in some disorder, he and his men found that some of their horses had disappeared and most of their equipment had been stolen. Three of the men were wounded, but all escaped, leaving behind five muskets, eleven swords, nineteen saddles, nine sets of horse armor, and a great deal of clothing and bedding. During the three days it had taken them to get back , they had almost starved to death but were saved by a woman they met on the plains who had given them some corn and beans.

Severely disappointed, Castaño began preparations for a punitive task force. The group set out the next morning, reaching Pecos early on the thirty-first. The villagers were waiting for them, with both men and women lined up on the roofs, ready for battle. Castaño spent the morning trying various forms of cajolery, but his efforts brought him nothing but the slings and arrows of outraged natives. In the early afternoon, he ordered a cannonball fired over the village, with no visible effect on its defenders, and the battle began.

The soldiers advanced on the village. As they fired their muskets, warriors began dropping from the roofs, only to be instantly replaced. Arrows and stones, the supplies of which were continually replenished by the women, rained down on the attackers. Nevertheless, the soldiers, protected by their armor and covered by the musketeers, began reaching roofs and driving the defenders back. By late afternoon, the villagers had all disappeared into their apartments, and the battle was over. To the few who remained visible to Castaño when he entered the village, he made conciliatory signs. In response they threw food down into one of the plazas. But they all stayed in their labyrinthine apartment house, foiling all attempts at capture. As darkness fell, Castaño posted a guard to catch any villagers who might try to leave and led his freebooters back to their camp outside the village for such New Year's Eve festivities as their circumstances would permit.

On New Year's Day, he visited the village and was gratified by the number of people who emerged from their apartments making signs of peace. Several soldiers, entering the apartment house with torches, searched through the many rooms and underground tunnels without finding any of the more retiring inhabitants. Castaño, impressed by the calm that had settled over the village, ordered the guards removed as night approached. As a result, by the next morning the village was completely deserted.

The visitors made themselves at home, raiding the vast stores for supplies of corn, beans, squash, vegetables, and chili seasoning, and sending back great quantities to the main body of would-be colonists. Castaño, having shown some mineral samples to a few villagers, who told him that such things could be found to the northwest (anyplace but *here*), ordered his advance party to prepare for a journey in that direction. This caused some grumbling among Castaño's party, because that route promised to take them through mountains over which the wagons could not follow; but the lure of gold, silver, and even copper quenched any sparks of mutiny.

Castaño and his highly mobile band spent the month of January 1591 investigating the many villages in the general area of what is now Santa Fe, New Mexico. He had no trouble with the inhabitants, who undoubtedly had heard the news from Pecos and, therefore, even endured a ceremony proclaiming them subjects of good King Philip. They may have enjoyed some aspects of this ritual, which was accompanied by much blowing of trumpets, firing of muskets, and kissing of crucifixes. Some of them were even appointed as officials of the new realm, with strange names like governor and mayor. It is highly unlikely that any of them had the faintest notion of what this was all about, but it may have provided many entertaining, if somewhat anxious, afternoons.

Late in January, the party returned to Pecos and led the main expeditionary group to the Rio Grande, where a colony was established near a village, which appears on New Mexico road maps today as the Santo Domingo Pueblo, halfway between Albuquerque and Santa Fe. At least Castaño reported to the viceroy that he had established a colony, but he was using the term very loosely to cover a collection of people and animals that promised to have about as much permanence as a traveling circus. One thing he did not do, despite some precedents, was to evict the inhabitants of the nearby village and replace them with his settlers. Pressure from his fellow colonists was enormous: the village offered ready-made shelter, and its residents constituted a large reservoir of slave labor. His resistance to this pressure might have cost him his life, if a plot to kill him had not been discovered and thwarted.

Not that death would have made much difference to Castaño in the coming days. While out on a gold hunt with a small party, he received word that a group of Spaniards had arrived and were waiting for him at headquarters. Assuming that they must be the additional colonists that he had requested from Mexico, he rushed back, only to be greeted by Captain Morlete, who had come with a couple of dozen cavalrymen to disperse the colony and take Castaño prisoner. In Mexico, he was eventually tried for illegal entry into New Mexico and exiled for six years to the Far East, where he died shortly before the arrival of a royal decree pardoning him and appointing him governor of New Mexico.

By the end of the sixteenth century, the royal spur for colonization finally reached some lower-level bureaucratic flanks. In the past, Spain's power in the New World had not been firmly established by its tentative probes and intermittent forays. Now that other European powers were beginning to show interest in North America, His Majesty would be delighted for them to find there an already flourishing and formidable establishment of Spanish colonies. This would require extensive, solidly implanted colonies of Spanish settlers—or, rather, Hispanic settlers, because ever more Spaniards, born in Mexico, considered themselves Mexicans—colonies of settlers fortified with a generous admixture of native laborers. To achieve this status, the king of Spain issued "encomienda," royal land grants, to colonists, providing them not only with portions of Rio Grande land but also with "the inhabitants thereof." Thus was born what came to be known as "the encomienda system," the closest thing to chattel slavery in North American history outside Dixieland. The river people had not been sold. They had been given away.

Juan de Oñate was a very wealthy man, probably one of the half-dozen wealthiest men in New Spain. His father had been a provincial governor in Mexico, and his wife traced her lineage, through the wife of the famed conqueror Cortés, to Montezuma. His family was influential, so his application to colonize New Mexico received special handling by the paper shufflers in Madrid. His wealth helped, too, because he was able to promise to underwrite all costs of the expedition, with the exception of the friars' expenses. Within months, instead of years, he received a royal charter. Ironically, in view of the peaceable nature of the Pueblos, the charter appointed him not only as the king's governor and captain-general but also as the "pacifier" of the provinces of New Mexico. This was underlined in a royal directive contained in the charter: "You will try to appeal to the natives with peace, friendship and kindness . . . and to persuade them to hear and accept the Holy Gospel."

Late in June 1598, in the southernmost of the Rio Grande villages, the people once again began making preparations for uninvited guests. This group, they had learned, was a formidable one: stretched out more than four miles in its progress along the river. (It included 130 families, some 70 single men, 83 wagons, and thousands of animals.) The villagers who preferred discretion to valor prevailed in the discussions, and as a result, the invaders were greeted with friendliness and ceremonies, and were even offered shelter. The visitors reciprocated by putting on a kind of jousting tournament to entertain the Pueblos and exhibit their proficiency in horsemanship and combat.

Shortly after these festivities were over, three of the villagers presented themselves to the governor, who was astonished to hear one of them exclaim, in the governor's language, "Thursday! Friday! Saturday! Sunday!" Distrusting his own ears, Oñate tried to get the man to repeat this rather obscure remark. The man refused, so Oñate, although he had brought along scads of trinkets and baubles with which to win over the natives, had all three men seized and threatened. Frightened, the talkative one cried out, again in Spanish, "Thomas and Christopher!" A crowd gathered amid excited efforts at more precise communication, chiefly through frantic signs in the air and feverish drawings on the ground.

Gradually, the man's meaning emerged. Castaño, in his rather unceremonious departure, had left behind at least two Mexicans who had been part of his expedition. These two men were still living at the village of Santo Domingo. Guessing that they must know Spanish and at least one Pueblo language, and therefore could act as interpreters, Oñate selected a force of about thirty cavalrymen and headed north. It seems likely that the Pueblos were up to their old tricks: find out what these people wanted and tell them about it, but be sure to steer them someplace else.

The next day the advance guard arrived at Puaray, where the soldiers had left the two friars after the brief invasion of 1581. The villagers received them well, offering gifts and lodging for the night. Inside the village, Oñate and a few companions noticed a painting which, under a thin coat of whitewash too hastily applied, unmistakably depicted the killing of two friars. Oñate signaled for no one to make any comment. Shortly after bedding down for the night, the invaders departed from the village in silence, in hot pursuit of Thomas and Christopher. Any urge to punish the Pueblos was outweighed by the more immediate requirement of interpreters.

Shortly thereafter, the accomplishsed liguists Thomas and Christopher were found at Santo Domingo. They explained that having been left behind by Castaño, the two had settled down in the village, married native women, and were living happily. It can be reasonably assumed that they wanted very much to stay there and continue enjoying their idyllic exis-

*Early engraving of Espanola, the pueblo Oñate
renamed and chose as his first colony.*

tence, but Oñate wanted them along as interpreters and so he
appropriated them. They were to prove extremely useful
interpreters in the days ahead.

Through his new interpreters, Oñate was able to call a
meeting of the chiefs of more than thirty of the villages in the
vicinity and to explain to them the new status of their people.
Having already, on the day he had entered New Mexico,
taken possession of absolutely everyone and everything, Oñate
invited them to submit to cross and crown peaceably. With an
eye on the heavily armed cavalry troop behind him, the native
leaders did so unquestioningly.

Having thus completed his work in Santo Domingo,
Oñate and his evangelical squadron hurried up the river to
make further disbursements from their inexhaustible cargo of
peaceful overtures. In the vicinity of present-day Espanola,

they came upon a magnificent, fertile valley nourished by two connecting rivers, the Rio Chama and the Rio Grande. This, Oñate decided, was the perfect place for his first colony. The ideal site for the town, it so happened, was already occupied by a native village. Providentially, this would save the colonists a great deal of hard work.

Oñate led the squadron into the village and called a meeting of the elders to explain the benefits of conquest. He told them that because the villagers were now subjects of His Most Christian Majesty, they must obey his commands or be severely punished. His first command was that they must immediately evacuate their homes in favor of the colonial horde that was soon to arrive to establish a colony. If the villagers showed any lack of eagerness in carrying out this order, they could expect encouragement from the cavalry, which doubtless looked very persuasive.

And so, as one historian has delicately put it, the people "peacefully evacuated their houses to let him and his soldiers move in." To memorialize his coup, Oñate named the village San Juan de los Caballeros, the Gentlemen's St. John. And to further enhance the prospects of the colony, he instructed the villagers to leave their personal belongings behind. They complied.

During the next month or so, the Christians gradually settled into their new home. It was a pleasant process, made easier by the neatness characteristic of the Pueblo's living habits and by delicious siestas during the long, warm summer afternoons. As the village filled up with arriving immigrants, however, it soon became inadequate to meet their needs, and Oñate decided to carry the message to a nearby town that looked large enough to accommodate the overflow. Once again, natives went out and colonists came in. One of the things Oñate found convenient about the process was its simplicity.

Since every respectable colony must have a capital, Oñate decided to build one, apparently as an addition to, or expansion of, his most recent urban acquisition. And since every respectable capital must have a cathedral, the Pueblo were introduced to yet another innovation, that of mass conscript labor. In less than a month, between August 11 and September 7, an irrigation ditch was dug from the river to the town, which was named San Gabriel. The ditch brought relief to parched throats, and a church was built to bring relief to parched souls. These achievements required massive indigenous help. Historians of the period put the number of native conscripts at 1,500—an incredible figure—implying that virtually all the able-bodied inhabitants of a considerable area were forced to leave their own daily work for at least four solid weeks in order to make the newcomers more comfortable. Arrangements like this were to become endemic in New Mexico and to be the subject of some of the conscripts' most bitter complaints. In this instance, as in most others to come, the village chiefs were then required to attend the interminable dedication ceremony in the new church, including the celebration of holy Mass.

The lack of native resistance to these particular events may be explained by the fact that the influence of village elders who recommended resistance was seriously undermined by an incident of a month or so earlier. The summer of 1598 had been a very dry one all along the river. The harvest was in danger, and the rain dances were taking on a tone of desperate urgency. Upon the arrival of the settlers, the friars, who had been informed of the need for rain, reassured the anxious natives that their prayers to the one true God would bring rain. Two days later, the skies provided an overwhelming downpour, the harvest was saved, and awestruck Pueblos spread the word that the friars possessed a power to be reckoned with. Unfortunately, it was a power whose unreliability was to become another source of disillusion and discontent in future years.

One of Oñate's first administrative acts as governor was to divide his territory of almost 90,000 square miles into seven ecclesiastical districts based generally on language groupings. Each district comprised several villages, and each had an assigned friar. The political divisions were similar, with each district to be ruled by a personal delegate of the governor. The chief priest in each village was instructed to appoint a native governor of the village each year whose chief duty was to act as a liaison officer, transmitting and enforcing the official regulations. The villagers would be permitted to govern themselves except when overruled by their overseers' demands, needs, desires, impulses, and whims.

Having thus wrapped things up administratively, Oñate turned his attention to the possibility of recouping some of the fortune he had spent on the invasion. The lure of treasure was still irrepressible. Not only was the fabled Quivira yet to be discovered, but somewhere to the west lay the Pacific Ocean, whose shores reputedly were laden with pearls of incalculable price. The governor had brought along two nephews, Vincente and Juan de Zaldivar, and he decided now to use them.

Vincente's assignment was to take a party of some sixty horsemen into the buffalo plains east of Pecos. Even if he couldn't find Quivira, or any other such deposits of treasure, he was to bring back buffalo for domestication. Vincente's small expedition started out in mid-September.

Juan's assignment was to fill in as acting governor in the absence of Oñate, who would soon be leaving on a much more extensive tour of the West. Upon Vincente's return, Juan was to relinquish the gubernatorial reins to him and start west to join Oñate. Early in October, Oñate started out with about a hundred calvarymen, first traveling to the southeast to investigate some salt deposits east of the Rio Grande, near present-day Estancia. These remnants of an ancient sea that once covered all the Southwest eventually proved to be an inexhaustible source of excellent salt for the colonists. The explorers then turned west, reaching the mesa-top village of Acoma late in October. At Acoma, Zutucapan, chief priest of the village, almost succeeded in ending Oñate's drive to colonize the Southwest.

Informed of the explorers' approach, Zutucapan called a war council to plan defensive action and extermination, if necessary. His son, however, and one of the elders, convinced the assembled warriors that resistance would be virtual suicide and that they should greet the intruders with as much friendliness as they could summon up. Zutucapan pretended to concede the point, but devised a plot to murder Oñate after they invited him into one of the kivas during the welcoming ceremonies. Unfortunately, the plan failed. Oñate wasn't interested in kivas. As soon as the formalities of submission were concluded, the governor hurried off to the west, extracting loyalty oaths from Zuni and Hopi villages along the way.

By early December, Oñate had found a few interesting mines but discovered no great riches, and he had no better notion of the whereabouts of the Pacific Ocean. Two or three bedraggled horsemen, returning from Zaldivar's expedition, brought him additional bad news. Vincente de Zaldivar had returned to San Gabriel early in November with neither gold nor buffalo. Quivira had proved as elusive as ever, and the captured buffalo had quickly "died of rage" in their corrals. A week or so after Zaldivar's return, Juan had left with thirty men, including Oñate's present news-bearers, but had met with disaster.

On December 1, Juan's party had arrived at Acoma and requested food. In response to Juan's request, the villagers explained that their supplies had been depleted by Oñate's demands, but, if he would bring his party up the 375-foot cliff to the village the next morning, they would give him what they could spare. Recognizing that the climb would be especially difficult and even hazardous in the gathering dusk, Juan agreed to wait until morning.

The next morning he and his men scrambled up the cliff, leaving behind only four men to guard the horses. At the top, they were warmly greeted by Zutucapan, who suggested that they go separately to the various houses and bring the provisions awaiting them there to a central plaza. Juan, who was only twenty-six and lacking military experience, agreed, and soon the soldiers were wandering about, separately and rather aimlessly, in the labyrinth formed by the village's narrow streets. This, of course, was Zutucapan's opportunity. He gave the signal, and hundreds of warriors attacked the soldiers with wooden spears and clubs, stone hatchets, and bows and arrows. Courage in battle was not lacking on either side. With sword and dagger, the soldiers gave a vigorous account of themselves in the fierce hand-to-hand fighting, which lasted for three hours. Juan de Zaldivar was felled three times only to rise and fight again, but the fourth time was his last. Only four of the soldiers in this battle lived to tell the tale. Forced back to the cliff, the Spaniards took the only gamble open to them and jumped some 300 feet into the soft sand below. The sand eased the impact of their fall, and they survived badly shaken but uninjured. This left eight survivors: the four soldiers who had been guarding the horses on the plain, and the four aerialists. They split into three groups to report to Vincente de Zaldivar in San Gabriel, to Oñate on the road, and to at least some of the lonely friars in their seven districts.

Oñate got back to San Gabriel in time for an unmerry Christmas and a series of conferences on what to do about Acoma. The local friars participated, assuring him that a punitive expedition against sky city fit comfortably into the ""just war" category but adding that any conversions should be by persuasion rather than physical violence—an afterthought that would prove to be highly superfluous. The consensus was that the soldiers' deaths would have to be avenged and that an example would have to be made of Acoma to prevent any spreading of such unsociability. And so, on January 21, 1599, the inhabitants of Acoma found themselves looking down on a force of seventy mounted soldiers led by Juan's brother Vincente.

Vincente called for their peaceful surrender. They declined the invitation, quite boisterously. The soldiers set up camp and settled down for the night. High above them the Acomans noisily built up their courage all night long. Their warriors outnumbered the soldiers by perhaps as much as ten to one; further, this was one village where horses could not be used. Yet the soldiers, with their glistening armor and deadly thundersticks, struck an almost mystical terror into native hearts, and Zutucapan barely managed to keep everyone at a fever pitch until the battle began.

The next day, after repeating his offer and hearing it

*Little had changed at the Acoma pueblo at the time this photograph
was taken by Edward S. Curtis in 1904, nearly four hundred years
after Oñate had attempted to colonize New Mexico.*

resoundingly rejected, Vincente ordered about fifty of his men
to make a conspicuous frontal attack by climbing the face of
the cliff. Meanwhile, he and eleven others crept up another
cliff in the rear and took the defenders totally by surprise, so
much so that the main force of attackers were given an opportunity to make it to the top and even to haul up a couple of

small cannons. The defenders, caught in a pincers, charged the new beachhead desperately but were cut down. Back and forth the battle raged, through the night and into the next day. Then Zutucapan was killed, and the fight went out of the remaining defenders. Quiet slowly settled over the smoldering ruins of the village, broken only by moans of the wounded, cries of the bereaved, and sporadic shouting as the soldiers executed unrepentant captives. Of the estimated 1,500 inhabitants of the now devastated village, only about 500 were still alive; of Vincente's force of seventy soldiers, sixty-eight survived. Small wonder that, after the battle, a group of frenzied village women were found wildly beating the dead body of their leader Zutucapan.

A week or so later, a grim yet triumphant cortege filed through the gates of San Gabriel: Vincente and his horsemen and hundreds of miserable, footsore captives. Within a few days, in something called a trial, Oñate announced the sentences: for all men over twenty-five years old, amputation of one foot and twenty years of slavery; for all other males and all females over twelve years old, twenty years of slavery; and for two Hopi men luckless enough to have been visiting at Acoma at the time of the rebellion, amputation of the right hand and release, to serve as a warning to their people.

Two of the captives managed to escape to the village of San Juan, where they took refuge in a kiva and for three days resisted all efforts to get them out. Finally, they asked for daggers with which to commit suicide. Oñate, reluctant to give them any weapons, instead ordered that hanging ropes be thrown down to them. To his surprise, the two men shortly came out of the kiva, climbed a large cottonwood nearby, and hanged themselves, with a bitter cry, "Our towns, our fields, our belongings are yours!"

Thus ended the war. Like earlier events, it illustrated a persistent dilemma faced by the conquistadors, who were awkwardly operating under two sets of practically contradictory orders from Madrid. One set, taken at face value by some historians of the conquest, instructed them to treat the natives humanely. The other instructed them to subjugate the land

and its people to His Majesty's imperial will, and to use whatever means was necessary. Of the two sets, the latter took precedence, both theoretically and practically, and was persistently given the benefit of any doubts. The former, at least from the natives' viewpoint, tended to evaporate in the heat of conquest.

Now that the Pueblos were "pacified" and San Gabriel was established—supported by its own crops and livestock as well as by a systematic despoiling of the surrounding villages—Oñate began getting restless again. In the summer of 1600 he dispatched Vincente to search again for the Pacific Ocean, but the mission was aborted by the terrain and by the natives, both proving impassable. About the only result of this expedition was the destruction of another village and the hanging of two of its chiefs.

That Christmas, Oñate received a present in the form of a caravan from Mexico bringing fresh colonists, including half a dozen friars, as well as clothing, hardware items, and of course plenty of arms with which to convert heathens. There were now about 500 Hispanic settlers in New Mexico. Oñate busied himself with a series of glowing reports to the king and the viceroy.

But the viceroy was also receiving some other, less glowing reports from one of Oñate's captains, a man whom the viceroy trusted and from whom he had secretly requested independent reports on the expedition's progress. This man reported that San Gabriel was little better than a slum, with its farming and grazing lands deteriorating because of Oñate's ceaseless treasure-hunting. The colonists, he continued, made themselves at home in the villages, helping themselves to whatever they wanted and enslaving the natives at will. Pueblos he described as gentle, inoffensive people subjected to outrageous treatment culminating in the excesses of the Acoma incident. Perhaps most damaging was his report that Oñate was behaving like a monarch and on at least one occasion had been addressed (by his nephew-crony, Vincente) as "Your Majesty."

His were probably not the only such reports finding their

way back to the viceroy. San Gabriel was experiencing a growing ferment of dissatisfaction. Many of the settlers felt betrayed by Oñate's promise of treasure, and the lack thereof. Others resented his neglect of the settlement. And some, drawing a distinction between Christendom and Christianity, were appalled by the treatment of Native Americans. Among these were some of the friars.

The reports created a considerable amount of dissension, of which the governor was evidently quite unaware. There has always been a good deal of bowing and scraping in Christendom, and the governor, like many executive types before and after him, doubtless found his portion completely reassuring. But the dissension, by giving his enemies at home some leverage, was the beginning of his downfall.

In the spring of 1601, some soldiers were attacked near the salt deposits to the southeast, and two of them were killed. In what by now might have been considered a conditioned reflex, Oñate sent a strong cavalry force, led by Vincente, to avenge their deaths by attacking the village of Quarai (the ruins of which today are a New Mexico state monument near the town of Mountainair). Although the troop sustained heavy casualties (including Vincente, whose arm was broken), the results were otherwise typical: 900 defenders died, 200 were captured, and the village was destroyed.

In June, having once again pacified the Pueblos, Oñate started out again, indomitably, in the direction of Quivira. In addition to some eighty men and a couple of friars, he took with him great quantities of the capital's food, about 700 horses and mules, and a goodly supply of native slaves to haul the luggage; this increased his popularity with nobody whatsoever. During his six-month absence, ferment among the San Gabriel settlers bubbled up into outright rebellion, and in September most of them left the colony and headed back for Mexico. And so it was that when the treasureless Oñate returned in late November, he found his capital almost deserted.

Meanwhile, in Madrid, Oñate was being investigated, and the government—despite the efforts of Vincente, who had been sent to Madrid by Oñate to plead his failing cause—

refused to drop another peso into the New Mexican colonial rathole. Oñate launched into a series of stratagems in an effort to maintain his position. He tried to get the deserters back from Mexico but was told that they had no legal obligation to return to San Gabriel. In the fall and winter of 1605-1606, he explored the West again in search of pearls from the ocean, as well as for a port through which to supply his colony; he got as far as the Gulf of California, mistaking it for the Pacific.

Even after his recall had been ordered by the king, Oñate managed to delay his return for more than two years. Finally, in 1609, he headed south for the last time, but before he reached the border his party was attacked by Native Americans and a soldier was killed—his only son. Thus bereaved and in disgrace, Oñate left the river to its decimated people. Fifteen years later, he received a royal pardon, and shortly thereafter he died.

Oñate left behind, in Madrid and Mexico, a heated controversy over whether to abandon the colonial effort or continue it. There was, of course, a good deal of talk about bringing the joys of Christianity to the natives. One friar reported that they were pathetically eager to embrace the holy faith, while another quoted them as saying that they could see no reason for joining a religion that brought with it so much suffering and violence. Such discussions kept the friars occupied while Madrid weighed the advantage of keeping the imperial presence alive in New Mexico as a token of its claim to the vast, unknown lands to the north. It was finally decided that the advantages were worth a further modest investment.

By 1600 the official character of New Mexico had changed quite abruptly. Treasure-hunting was out, colonizing was in. Oñate's successor, a don named Peralta, showed no interest whatsoever in the mysteries of Quivira or in oceanic pearls. Instead, upon taking office he limited his touring to the area around San Gabriel in search of a better site for the colonial capital. He found one on a tributary of the Rio Grande, in the foothills of the Sangre de Cristo Mountains. Here, he announced, he would build a town to be named

Sante Fe in honor of the holy faith. Of course he wouldn't build it himself, nor would his few colonists build it themselves. There were many native hands available to make work light for the settlers. Beyond the building of Santa Fe, however, there would never really be enough hands available for the grandiose undertakings of *both* church and state. The division of native labor was to be the subject of a stimulating institutional quarrel over the coming years, with the settlers as its participants and the Pueblos as its victims.

The move from San Gabriel to Santa Fe took place in the latter part of 1610, after a hot summer of slave labor had produced an aqueduct to carry water through the new capital, a large "palace" for the governor fronting on a spacious plaza, a cathedral, and houses for the settlers. And now that the province had a respectable capital, the next move was to assure that the capital would soon have a respectable province. This meant bringing in more colonists for the crown and more friars for the cross.

By 1624 the governor of Santa Fe was able to report that the number of colonists had reached 2,000, and six years later the Franciscan superior general of the province informed the king from his headquarters in Santo Domingo that some sixty friars were establishing the faith in about ninety villages, having baptized around 60,000 people. The conquest of the river people was now essentially complete. The mailed fist had become the upper hand.

Haciendas grew up along the river, north and south of Santa Fe. They were not unlike the plantations of a later culture, a thousand miles to the east: oases of gracious living enjoyed by a supervisory elite and nourished by the sweat of other brows. The encomienda system was now solidly established, and each hacienda had its corps of Indian serfs to till the fields, maintain the livestock, tend the house, and make whatever the master wanted to eat, to wear, or to sell in the growing trade with Mexico. Gone was the placid life that Pueblos had known a hundred years before.

Although the natives served the haciendas, most of them lived at home, in their villages. Here they might have expected some rest and relief, but two aspects of the encomienda system denied them even this. In the first place, they no longer had enough time to keep their fields in good repair or even work with them very much. Thus, despite their desperate overtime work, they were reduced to a chronic state of destitution that depleted their energies, injured their health, and destroyed what little independence they had left. In the second place, they had to contend with the friars.

About a hundred years earlier, the pope in Rome had condemned the proposition that the natives of the American continents were nothing more than beasts of burden furnished to Christians for their comfort by a solicitous Providence; as human beings, they were not to be deprived of their liberty or property. But the pope's words, like so many papal words, rang hollow amid the examples of luxurious amorality set by Vatican authorities. Furthermore, Rome fervently supported missionary activity in the Americas, showing much more interest in numbers of conversions than in methods of conversion. By the time its interest reached the humble friar in the boondocks, through layers of governmental and ecclesiastical officials, it had become much more aggressive in tone. The American natives were heathen savages who worshipped devils and would spend eternity suffering the tortures of hell unless they were saved, one way or another.

The Spanish missionaries had not come from a land of pluralistic tolerance. They believed in eternal salvation through baptism, and in eternal damnation without it. Baptizing someone in the true faith, even forcibly, was considered an incomparable act of love, because it could save that soul from an eternity of excruciating torment and provide, instead, an opportunity for everlasting ecstasy.

Thus the ceremonies during which the natives were baptized included a genuine joy, at least among the friars and others thoroughly committed to gathering in the sheaves. And by the same token, any native resistance to conversion was considered the work of Satan's devils, the friars' tireless adversaries in the ceaseless competition for souls. Such resistance therefore had to be exorcised by any means available, and this led to a perpetual pitched battle between the forces of good and of evil. And the casualty rate, as the natives could testify, was generally hardest on those in the middle.

Despite the friars' glowing reports of numerous baptisms, Christianity among the Pueblos was never much more than an accommodation, motivated by uncertainty and fear of the frightful punishments awaiting them in this world and perhaps in the next as well. In the late nineteenth century an anthropologist, after an intensive study of Pueblo culture, asserted that the people were no more Christian than they had been before the conquest. In the middle of the seventeenth century, if the friars required that they go through the officially approved motions, then the Pueblos would go through the motions, for they knew that behind the friars stood soldiers. But they had the courage and the dedication necessary to continue practicing their own religion in their kivas, as secretly as possible but regularly and frequently. When the friars caught on, they became embroiled in a controversy over whether to tolerate it or take arms against it. Because the controversy was never resolved, each friar was generally left to make his own decision.

Institutional religions have classically been given to the building of monumental meeting places, usually in the form of temples and churches, and ecclesiastical activity along the Rio Grande was no exception. Because each village had to have its own church, Pueblos had to devote long, hard hours to heavy construction work, learning new techniques of architectural engineering, as well as lifting and hauling, in the service of the new symbolism. The churches were no little, makeshift affairs. They ran as much as a hundred feet long by forty feet wide by sixty feet high, with thick walls of stone or adobe, and roofs supported by enormous timbers dragged laboriously from high mountains miles away. In addition, another large building had to be provided for the living quarters of the friar and his servants, with perhaps a small chapel and a reading room and other domestic amenities. After all this had been built, it had to be maintained, and beyond that there was always plenty of work to be done in the gardens and orchards and vineyards. Indeed, there was so much work to be done that the friars soon began to complain about the demands made on their flocks by the haciendas. The settlers responded in kind, and before long the nasty quarrel was being carried on at the most exalted levels.

From about the turn of the century, the quarrel kept growing in intensity but was pretty well confined to tattletale complaints in the reports that went to the harassed viceroy with each returning caravan. As early as 1612, however, it surfaced quite spectacularly. The first act of the drama took place in the northern village of Taos, where Governor Peralta's armed and mounted tax collectors arrived one day to extract the customary tribute from the villagers. Before the villagers could comply, a friar strode up and informed the soldiers in loud and unmistakable terms that they would not be given so much as a single bean. This was Fray Isidro Ordonez, the Franciscan superior general, a man whose reputation was as odious as his credentials were suspect. The soldiers, who of course wouldn't have tolerated this from a native but who shared the prevailing reverence for clerics, turned tail for Santa Fe. Fray Ordonez got there not long after they did, demanding to see Peralta. The governor, having talked with his frustrated revenue agents, was just as eager to see Ordonez. The two met head-on. Peralta yelled at the friar: the governor's men were not to be prevented from doing their duty. Ordonez yelled back: that duty was nothing less than extortion, a theft of what belonged to the church. For giving such orders, Peralta was thereby excommunicated.

The governor didn't like such personal abuse. He whipped out a pistol and fired at Ordonez, missing him completely but winging a couple of bystanders. Ordonez demanded of the town-council members present that they throw the governor out of office, but they refused to get involved. Infuriated, Ordonez strode into the church and a moment later reappeared with the Governor's Chair, which he cast out rudely upon unhallowed ground. Then he issued a solemn ecclesiastical order: no one was to carry any message from the governor to Mexico, on pain of excommunication and a charge of treason.

Peralta, finding himself outmaneuvered, soon set out for Mexico with a small party, to report to the viceroy in person. He and his friends got as far as Isleta, where they were overtaken by soldiers from the all-pervasive Inquisition. Not long thereafter, Peralta was enjoying the rather meager comforts of a Santa Fe jail. His adversary's victory was brief. In reply to the contentious friar's reports of the controversy, the viceroy replaced them both.

During the first eighty years of the seventeenth century, New Mexico was ruled, more or less, by a succession of more than twenty governors. The post was generally considered as a splendid business opportunity, offering quick profits to a go-getter with a knack for extortion and for trafficking in slaves. As military dictator and police chief of the province, responsible only to a preoccupied authority more than a thousand rugged miles away, the governor could rake off a substantial percentage of all agricultural and commercial production from both the haciendas and the native villages, and of course regularly did. The judicial system, with its capricious verdicts and harsh penalties, provided a steady, if limited, supply of slaves, periodically augmented by captives taken in punitive raids on the villages and in expeditions against Navajos and Apaches. It is hardly surprising that, during these eighty years, a large proportion of Pueblos—probably more than half—simply disappeared. Most of the refugees who survived joined other native groups, to some extent the Apaches but more especially the Navajos. One effect of this migration can be seen today in the similarities between Navajo and Pueblo cultures.

From the average governor's viewpoint, the Franciscans' missionary effort was at best a monumental nuisance. In 1619 a governor named Eulate, in an attempt to loosen the friars' hold on the villages, issued an order permitting, and indeed encouraging, a revival of native religious rituals. The response of the villagers was immediate and enthusiastic: the kachinas and koshare emerged from the secrecy of the kivas, prayer sticks reappeared, sacred cornmeal again was sprinkled, and the people once again were dancing in the streets and plazas. And native priests, who of course had always been among the friars' implacable opponents, were restored in some measure to their former positions.

Apparently, the friars, in general, reacted just as Eulate had hoped and expected. Like Moses returning from Mount Sinai, they stormed and thundered, and fumed and railed against this resurgence of merry deviltry. Some of them set kivas on fire, tossing ceremonial dress, masks, and other works of the devil into the purging flames. But such damage could be repaired, and without soldiers behind them the missionaries were essentially helpless. Indeed, their sudden exhibition of heated intolerance simply alienated the Pueblos further, perhaps beyond Eulate's intentions.

This imaginative innovation of Eulate's set the pattern to be followed by most of his successors, escalating the church-state war to a desperate level. The record of this period is heavily seasoned with libelous charges and countercharges. Pueblo east of the river, the friars complained, were used as beasts of burden to haul great, backbreaking sacks of salt for the delectation of government officials in Santa Fe. Others were whipped for singing at mass, and still others were threatened with whipping for rendering any service to the friars. And in every village the outlawed Pueblo dances continued, egged on by devilish anticlericals. The governors responded to such charges in kind. They complained that the friars lived in luxurious comfort, attended by hosts of slaves. They drank. They fornicated. They punished the natives brutally for minor infractions. They whipped them for missing mass. And so on. Either way, it seems, the chief impression that the villagers gained from all this came from the business end of a whip.

In 1637 Don Luis de Rosas was appointed governor. A really ambitious troublemaker, he incited the Pueblos against the friars so persuasively that the friar at the village of Jemez was murdered and, at Taos, the friar was killed and the church destroyed. In 1641 Don Luis was fortuitously, and perhaps clerically, assassinated. That year brought the Pueblos still another evil of civilization—an epidemic of the white man's disease smallpox. Thousands died.

A decade later, Governor Lopez publicly approved of

Pueblo religious ceremonies, insisting that they be performed for him on his official visits to the villages. This conduct aroused the interest of the Holy Office of the Inquisition in Mexico City, and he was removed from office in 1660.

The next governor, a man named Penalosa, was pompous and egotistical. As he and his retinue approached the river villages after leaving El Paso, he sent messengers ahead to demand that a large and mobile welcoming committee meet him near Socorro and conduct him to Santa Fe. As he traveled up the river he insisted that each village entertain him with a costly display of its affection and its delight at his appointment. Once in Santa Fe, he demanded that each week a native musician from another village come to play a flute during his meals. This proved to be only the first of many such requests.

The Franciscan superior-general at this time, a strong-minded man named Posada, took advantage of the governor's preccupation with his self-importance to reestablish the old form of Christianity among the Pueblo. Hurriedly dispatching orders to all the villages, he instructed the friars to purge their parishes of all Native American religious customs, symbols, and artifacts. The friars, with the aid of soldiers, managed to break into the kivas by the dozen, utterly destroying the images and artifacts they had been railing against for so many frustrating years. In the process, they apparently also destroyed the remnants of the gentler image of Christianity that had been created among some of the villagers in the earlier missionary days. Mutterings of revolt rustled throughout the land. Bitter seeds had been sown in aching hearts, although the harvest was still almost a generation away.

When Penalosa finally realized what was going on, he renewed the church-state battle with a series of anticlerical decrees and some very pointed official acts. When the superior-general, Posada, appointed a friar to restore the ravaged church at Taos, for example, Penalosa in turn appointed, as the new governor of the village, the man most responsible for the death of the friar's predecessor and for the destruction of the church. Further, he warned the villagers that anyone who helped restore the church would be executed.

When Posada, who was visiting Pecos at the time, heard the news, he sent a message to Santa Fe directing Penalosa to cease and desist or suffer pain of excommunication. The governor, fuming that there wasn't anyone in New Mexico with enough authority to excommunicate him, dispatched a squad to Pecos, where the superior-general was apprehended, forcibly returned to Santa Fe, and placed under house arrest in the governor's palace. That did it. As an official of the Inquisition, Posada managed to get a smoldering report of the incident to Inquisition headquarters in Mexico City, and before long Penalosa was on his way back to Mexico to pay the penalties, which included exile from the western hemisphere. New troubles were now in store for the river people.

CHAPTER THREE
REVOLT
AND
RECLAMATION

You may as well attempt to convert the Jews without the Inquisition as to convert Indians without soldiers.
Don Diego de Vargas (1693)

BY 1660, there were about 2,500 Hispanics living along the river amid perhaps ten times as many Native Americans. Among the latter there always had been a strong minority urging the people to rise up against their oppressors and banish them from the land. If the people had been united by a common language, a forceful military leadership, and a singleness of resolve, they might have done just that.

But among the majority, bitter, frightening memories were still strong. The villagers of Acoma, for example, once had listened to an insurrectionist minority, and their village had been utterly destroyed. There was also the question of alternatives, for the invaders' military innovations at least had brought the river people some protection against the nomads of the plains. And finally, the Christian gods seemed to have brought a long period of fertility to the land, providing an abundance of precious water to nourish the life-giving crops.

Around 1660, however, both that protection and the providence began a long period of decline. Drought settled on the land, not only along the river but throughout the

Southwest. The hot sun, blazing in cloudless skies, seared and cracked the dusty earth, killing the livestock, shriveling the crops, and stunting vegetation. Stores of food from happier times dwindled rapidly, and soon the people could see the hollow stare of hunger in their children's eyes.

This famine was the worst they had ever known, for it was severely aggravated by the widespread policy of sharing, which the hungry settlers observed with a vengeance. The starving were forced to share with the merely hungry, and thousands of Pueblos died in their villages, victims of famine, disease, and debilitating economic transfusions. In 1680 there were still about 2,500 foreign settlers in New Mexico, as there had been in 1660 when the drought began.

Then other killers struck. From out of the north and east, the Navajos and the Apaches descended once again, forced by their desperate hunger to brave the lethal weapons of the Spaniards in search of food. But now the weakened settlers had all they could do to defend themselves. The Pueblos, weakened not only by famine but also by their years under the foreign heel, were vulnerable to the raiders' attacks as they had never been before. Thousands more died, not only in defense of their pitiful resources but also as a result of being robbed of those resources. The raiders indulged in mass killings far beyond the requirements of armed robbery. Although they had not caught on to the invader's trick of destruction by fire, they made life so miserable for Pueblos that many of the villages were soon abandoned. East of the river, along the edge of Apache country, a long line of village ruins remains today, identified as "The Cities That Died of Fear."

Adversity promotes religion if not ethics. Pueblos were remorsefully returning to their ancient gods in droves. The colonists, too, examined their consciences and arrived at a singular conclusion: they had incurred the displeasure of God by being too lenient with the heathens and by interfering with the friars' mission of stamping out all vestiges of Pueblo religion. This gave the colonial community a reason for reconciling their differences and healing old wounds.

So church and state patched up their quarrel under a governor named Trevino, who reissued the old prohibitions against native rituals, branding them as witchcraft and idolatry. As part of his campaign, he dispatched platoons of soldiers to arrest Pueblo ringleaders in the villages—the chief priests, the priests of the native sodalities, the medicine men—and parade them back and forth to Santa Fe for trial and punishment. The trial was routine and the punishment severe. Four of the victims, accused of casting a spell on a friar, were ceremonially hanged. The others, after a public horsewhipping, were imprisoned. Among them was a chief priest named Popé. His name (pronounced pope-*pay*) was destined to become a household word among the colonists.

The governor's public humiliation of high-ranking Pueblo priests was meant, of course, to break the back of any native resistance that might interfere with the propagation of the Christian faith. What it actually did, however, was to galvanize and unify that resistance. The governor had his first taste of organized impertinence when no less than seventy Pueblo leaders appeared before his palace one morning, demanding an audience. Apparently, there was something in their demeanor that prompted him to grant it at once: a quiet determination, a grim resolve. They did not demand, they informed. They said that the people could not live without the forty-three men he had imprisoned. Either they would be released, or the Pueblos would abandon all their villages, leaving the settlers to their own devices. Further, most of them would probably join the Navajos and the Apaches, who, because of the persistent slave raids, were now the Spaniards bitter, implacable enemies. This would put the villagers in a position to wage all-out war and purge their land of the intruders. The choice was his.

The governor was short of soldiers (he had less than a dozen in Santa Fe), and what soldiers he had were short of arms and ammunition. He needed no electronic computers to weigh the overwhelming numerical odds, and he could recognize determination when he saw it. He opted for release of the prisoners.

Popé returned to his village of San Juan with the scars of

Popé came to this seven-story pueblo of San Juan in 1680 to plan the revolt that successfully drove the Spaniards from New Mexico.

whips upon his back and hatred in his soul. He had always been a troublemaker, a rebel, a leading advocate of purging the river of foreign poison. He was now fanatic, single-minded, and relentless. He also had a reputation as an effective war chief, and this enhanced his influence as the thoughts of the river people turned more and more to war. Under his guidance their unity was growing every day. In a show of power, he moved his headquarters to a kiva in Taos because that village was a bit more conveniently located. He had even begun recruiting lieutenants —Catiti of Santo Domingo, Jaca of Taos, Tupatu of Picuris. The conspiracy spread slowly, taking five long years to come to fruition, but at the end of each of those years, it was stronger than it had been at the beginning.

During the spring and summer of 1680, the pace of the conspiracy accelerated. The tentative feelers that Popé had cautiously advanced in the early years had now become a network of firm commitments. Under the triple burden of persistent famine, hard labor, and proselytizing, the incentive for rebellion had waxed, not waned, with the passage of time. Patience and long-suffering had run their course, and for Popé the moment for the fateful decision was at hand.

That decision was complicated by the need for secrecy; Popé was quite aware of the vital importance of surprise. His communications network was restricted to priests and warriors, who would have to provide leadership and do the fighting. Information was withheld from the women and children and from all men whose sympathies were suspect. Among the leaders of every village were lackeys of the colonists. The village governors, for instance, had not earned their appointment by the colonial governor by exhibiting a spirit of brazen independence, and there were others who had genuine doubts about the practical wisdom of rebellion. In Popé's own village of San Juan, his son-in-law had grown rich and powerful by cooperating with the colonial authorities. Anxious to discourage any would-be traitors, Popé accused him of espionage and managed to have him stoned to death.

Yet the rebel leader knew that the probability was high that information would be leaked to the foreigners. Not only would this telegraph the blow, but it also would make it much harder for him to so organize things that all the villages would revolt at the same time. So he devised a plan. (This is one interpretation of the historical record; the other leaves much more to blind chance.) Having somewhat arbitrarily chosen August 13 as D-day, Popé began informing his fellow chief conspirators early in August. To the various villages he sent loosely knotted ropes (a popular counting device among the Pueblos) from which a knot was to be removed each morning; the day of the last knot would be the day for the revolt. But in addition, he warned them to keep themselves and their warriors ready, for if he found that the foreigners had been alerted he might have to move the date up by several knots, in which case he would let them know by special messengers. His foresight was to prove invaluable. It was certainly much more helpful than another kind of foresight to which he laid claim—a mystical clairvoyance that brought him such experiences as the dream in which he saw the settlers being washed away in a torrent of their own blood.

Throughout the summer in Santa Fe, reports of rebellious plotting had filtered in to Governor Otermin, but they had seemed no more alarming than other rumors that had been floating around for years. On August 9, however, he received the same report from five separate sources warning him that the northern villages were scheduled to revolt on the thirteenth and that other villages were expected to follow suit shortly thereafter. Although still not seriously alarmed, Otermin did take the precaution of alerting the missions and haciendas along the river, instructing the people to the north to assemble at Santa Fe at the first signs of rebellion, and the people to the south to assemble at Isleta.

Popé had his informers too, of course. Once told of the governor's precautions, he dispatched his special messengers, advancing D-day to August 10, a Saturday.

At dawn that morning, in the village of Tesuque, nine miles north of Santa Fe, the friar was at the altar when some of his parishioners burst into the church, formidably armed and wearing their war paint. "What is this, children?" he reportedly cried out. "Have you gone insane? I will help you. I will die a thousand times for you." The warriors murdered him, broke the statues, defaced the paintings, and set the church on fire. As so it went, with minor variations, at most of the northern villages before the weekend was over: the friars killed, the images and vestments and other sacred things destroyed, the churches gutted. Haciendas became slaughterhouses, whole families falling victim to Pueblo retribution. The rebellion was spreading like the desert wind. From San

Juan and Taos in the north to Santo Domingo in the south, from Pecos in the east to Acoma and Zuni in the west, friars were dying, churches were being destroyed, and the Rio Grande people were in command.

From haciendas in the vicinity of Santa Fe, refugees poured into the capital, more than a thousand of them. The plaza and its surrounding buildings, forming a walled garrison, were soon packed with people, horses, and livestock. Otermin ordered the gates locked. Although the governor had recently been sent some reinforcements, he still had only seventy-five soldiers and seventy-five other armed men to defend the garrison against the inevitable Pueblo attack. Tensely, expectantly, the assemblage waited through the weekend. On Monday the infiltration of the outlying parts of the town began, and by Tuesday morning more than 500 painted warriors, many of them on horseback carrying foreign weapons, were roaming about and occasionally conducting brief war dances around the besieged garrison.

The governor, after ordering that his two brass cannons be brought to the wall and aimed at the main body of besiegers, requested negotiations, offering safe conduct to any of them who would enter the garrison and discuss the situation. The warriors chose a Spanish-speaking man who the governor knew had been baptized and whom he had always considered friendly. The man entered the garrison on horseback, and Otermin immediately began dressing him down with questions. Had he taken leave of his senses? How could he behave this way against his patient, generous, kind and loving friends? And so on. Ignoring this stream of interrogatory insults, the man stolidly held out before him two small crosses, one red and one white. The governor, he explained dispassionately, must choose one. If he chose the white, there would be no more killing, but all the settlers would have to return to Mexico at once; they would not be molested during their departure. If he chose the red, indicating that the settlers intended to stay, then all would be killed. Otermin, after upraiding the man for abandoning his Christian faith, refused to have anything to do with his crosses, and the man rode back out of the garrison.

Although Pueblo warriors outnumbered Otermin's fighting men by about three to one, the governor had good reason to believe that the odds would soon grow worse, with the arrival of heavy reinforcements already on their way from the more distant villages. Now, he and his captains decided, would be a good time to sashay out and strike a blow for freedom. A small group was ordered to make a dash out of the gate, take up positions of reasonable cover, and smite the rebels hip and thigh. Out they went, and they smote furiously, but the incorrigible rebels smote right back. Before long Otermin himself led a larger force out of the garrison, and the smiting became extraordinary indeed. It raged on all day, until nightfall drew a merciful veil over the distinction between friend and foe. The two sides retired for rest and repair.

During the night and next day, Wednesday, another 1,500 warriors arrived. Why the full force of 2,000 failed to rush the garrison from all sides and simply overwhelm it was a puzzle to the defenders and is still a puzzle to historians today. The old problem of disunity among the river people is a possible but not very likely explanation, in view of the unity being displayed in the rebellion. A charge of cowardice in battle cannot be squared with the historical record. One explanation that does square with what we know about the character of the Pueblo, and incidentally with their red-cross/white-cross ultimatum, is that they were great believers in limited objectives and limited risks. They were not a bloodthirsty people. All they wanted was for the interlopers to go away. Despite their pent-up resentment, they preferred a unilateral exodus to bilateral slaughter.

This viewpoint exhibited itself in the warriors' next move. By Thursday morning, the fifteenth, further reinforcements had swelled the attacking force to about 2,500. If the settlers had any idea of breaking out of their trap and heading south, that idea was now dead. Their only alternative was to wait for the warriors' all-out assault, or a miraculous rescue from the south. But neither the assault nor the rescue ever came. On Friday the warriors cut off the garrison's water supply; and, despite some valiant attempts by Otermin's soldiers to retake the ditch, the water stayed cut off. Occasionally a band of warriors would rush the garrison, raking it with gunfire and arrows and at one point setting the church on fire. They even captured the two cannons, but only briefly. By nightfall nearly every fighting man in the garrison had been wounded, including the governor. The town outside the garrison was almost totally on fire, and over the crackling of the flames could be heard voices singing Latin hymns in bitter mockery.

On Sunday morning, the eighteenth, the defenders were desperate. Some of the livestock had died, or were dying of thirst, and this brought the dreaded danger of an epidemic. Thoroughly alarmed, Otermin led his entire force out of the garrison in a sudden and unexpected onslaught, and the warriors, after losing about 300 killed and forty-seven captured, retreated into the surrounding hills. They could afford to wait and see what happened, in the hope that Otermin would eventually choose the white cross of bloodless retreat.

He did. His interrogations of the captives convinced him that the Pueblo were unified beyond his most pessimistic estimates and that they meant business beyond his most harrowing fears. All foreign presence in the north had simply been eliminated. The situation in the south evidently was not much better, with the haciendas abandoned and the survivors presumably assembled at Isleta. His discussion with his captains and the friars in the garrison led to a clear consensus: the only thing to do was to leave in the hope of joining the Isleta refugees. Once there, they could all decide what further action to take. For now the only other thing to do was to execute their forty-seven hapless captives.

On August 21, the long line of a thousand refugees, with 400 head of livestock and a couple of wagons, emerged from the garrison, wended its way through the ruins of Santa Fe, and began its eighty-mile trek to Isleta. The pace was glacial; there were so few horses that even some of the lame had to walk, and no one was to be left behind. From the crests of the hills the warriors looked down at the long column impassively, their silence broken, in a sense, only by their smoke signals announcing the departure to contingents further south. The

*During the Pueblo revolt, many Catholic churches were
destroyed. Today, ruins still remain of the Pecos
Mission Church at Pecos Pueblo, New Mexico.*

travelers continued on their way unmolested. They were leaving now, and the warriors had no reason to attack them.
Apparently the Pueblos did not have a god of vengeance.

The eighty-mile trip took six grueling days to complete.
All along the way, the refugees passed grim signs of the revolt:
ruined haciendas, destroyed missions, decomposing bodies of
friars and settlers. They met only two lone Native Americans,
on separate occasions. To the first, Otermin addressed a puz-

zled question: why on earth had the natives rebelled? The people were exhausted, the man replied, by the work they had been forced to do for the colonists, who left them no time to support themselves. To the second, an ancient fellow reportedly over eighty, Otermin addressed the same question and received a different but by no means contradictory answer. The colonists, the old man said, had tried to rob the river people of their religious beliefs and customs, which had stood them in good stead for untold generations. Ignoring this reply, Otermin then asked about the settlers at Isleta. Yes, they had gathered there, the old man answered, but after a while they had left the village, disappearing southward, down the valley. This Otermin believed, and with dismay.

On August 27 the old man's story was confirmed. The column arrived at Isleta, and no one was there. Otermin was indignant. His instructions to Lieutenant General Garcia had been to wait at Isleta for the settlers from the north. This was a fine welcome for his exhausted travelers. He immediately sent four mounted men south to find Garcia and tell him to hold his horses. Wherever he was, he was to halt his refugees on the spot and then come back himself and report to his governor and captain-general. The messengers found Garcia & Co. at a point along the river near Socorro. They gave him the message. The company stopped. Garcia returned.

He was prepared to face the music with some tunes of his own. Wise in the ways of autocratic bureaucracy, he brought along a saddlebagful of written testimonials, signed and sealed, demonstrating his wisdom and good faith. He had not received any instructions from Otermin, he explained; the assembling at Isleta had simply seemed the most sensible thing to do. He had tried to get word to Santa Fe, but no messengers had been able to get through. Refugees who had managed to stagger down to Isleta had reported that, in the north, everyone and everything Hispanic had been destroyed. Under the circumstances, he and the other leaders of *his* thousand refugees had opted for the better part of valor.

Otermin, appeased by the man's eloquence and documentation, pardoned him for doing what was so obviously sensible, and the journey resumed. Shortly thereafter, a party of about forty cavalrymen appeared. They were from El Paso, and they had come to escort the 2,000 refugees. By early October they were all living in camps around El Paso, in safety if not in luxurious comfort. At least they had been luckier than the 400 Christians who had lost their lives in the uprising, though perhaps not so lucky as the hundred or so who seem to have escaped entirely. Most of the refugees wanted desperately to forget all about New Mexico. Mexico was close now and irresistibly inviting. To put it simply, they wanted out.

The friars, however, led by a man named Ayeta, the Franciscan quartermaster for New Mexico, could not accept withdrawal from so fertile a missionary field. The friars knew, without conducting an opinion poll, that the refugees really didn't know what was good for them. For if they did leave New Mexico permanently, there would be no reason for the government to station soldiers there; and without soldiers, how could the friars propagate the Holy Faith? But to all such cogent arguments the ex-settlers replied most firmly: they wanted out. And so Ayeta played a neat little trick on them.

El Paso was in the Mexican province of New Biscay. Thus, the refugees were outside the jurisdiction of Governor Otermin of New Mexico, who agreed with the friars about the necessity of returning the river colony to its former happy status. Ayeta arranged with the governor of New Biscay and the viceroy to declare El Paso to be officially a part of New Mexico until further notice. As a result, it was now under Otermin's authority, including the hapless refugees.

But the river people were free at last, free to cultivate their own fields, sing their own songs, pray their own prayers, live their own lives. Whether they would still know what to do with freedom remained to be seen.

CHAPTER FOUR

RECONQUEST AND COLONIZATION

A more upright and useful people are nowhere to be found.

A GOVERNMENT AGENT IN SANTA FE
(LATE NINETEENTH CENTURY)

THE INTRUDERS were gone at last. To all outward appearances, the Pueblos now had every opportunity for a renaissance of their ancient culture. The Spaniards had assaulted that culture vigorously, if intermittently, over the past century and a half. Now the next decade would demonstrate that they had also done something else: they had corrupted its very fiber.

The corruption showed itself most conspicuously in the conduct of the old priest-warrior, Popé, who at once began acting much more like a European warlord than the leader of a people with an age-old tradition of government by consent. His delusions of grandeur are understandable enough: in all the 500-year history of European trespassing in the New World, he was to be the only Native American leader ever to throw the invaders out. Yet a contemplation of his story is an exercise in disappointment, for he cleared the stage of strutters only to strut on it himself.

First he issued a series of parapapal bulls designed to exorcise the imported religion from the lives of the river people. The Christian god, he declared, had been made of rotten wood and was dead at last. All vestiges, all reminders of it must be obliterated. All the churches still standing must be razed. Not a single cross must exist in the river lands, not a single statue, not a single paten or chalice. Not a single word of that hated foreign tongue, with its harsh imperative mood, must ever be heard again, including Christian names—no more Juans or Pedros or Rosas or Marias. And everyone must cleanse himself or herself of the stain of baptism with the traditional symbolic suds of the yucca plant.

Kivas, he declared, were back in fashion, as were the dances, the kachinas, the masks and costumes, and the koshare. The changeover was to be complete. Even the good things that the settlers had brought—fruit orchards, livestock, horses—would have to be abandoned. (The release of the horses brought generations of mustangs to the plains and mobility to countless native warriors throughout the virgin West.) All these edicts of Popé's were, in general, enthusiastically obeyed. Christianity, for all the wistful sighs rising from the unemployed missionaries in El Paso, can hardly be said to have won the hearts of the people.

Yet the very fact that Popé alone was issuing these orders kept alive the European innovation most thoroughly foreign to the culture of the river people: the notion of authority by divine right, of religious and political authority received directly from the gods rather than through the people. To add supernatural resonance to his authoritarian pronouncements during the long years of plotting the revolt, Popé had stressed his intimacy with various dignitaries of the spirit world. Now that he had the opportunity to lead the Pueblos, the idea of a single governor ruling over all the river people appealed to him. Setting himself up in the palace in Santa Fe, he reintroduced many of the customs that he had schemed and fought so hard to eradicate: the bowing and scraping, the centralization of power, government by whim, the payment of tribute, and the enslavement of nonconformists.

In the past, if old war leaders had brought peace and prosperity to the river people, their ambitions might have been tolerated. But now, despite the renewal of the rain dances and other prayers of desperate petition, the drought continued unabated. The raids of the starving nomads from the plains grew worse, and some Pueblos even began to prey upon their own people. Dozens of villages were abandoned, especially south of Santo Domingo. Evil portents abounded; a shock of fear ran through the remaining towns as the news spread that during a dance Catiti, one of Popé's chief lieutenants, had suddenly dropped dead.

Eroded by adversity, the unity of the uprising gradually dissolved. Even within the northern group of towns the discontent grew so acute that a revolt broke out, briefly replacing Popé with another of his chief lieutenants, Tupatu. Finally, after regaining his precarious throne for a few more miserable years, Popé died in 1688. Once again the more rational Tupatu took command, but much too late. Popé, for all his communion with the spirit world, had failed to stem the tide of dissolution. The land of the river people was a shambles. Already it was ripe for reconquest.

Shortly after the colonists had been thrown out of New Mexico, Fray Ayeta traveled to Mexico City, where he was shown a royal edict, just then arrived, to the effect that the colonists must not allow themselves to be thrown out of New Mexico. On the strength of this edict, the viceroy assigned Ayeta to take a new supply caravan, complete with some new colonists and soldiers, back to El Paso. The friar was only too glad to comply, for he knew that only a reconquest could restore the poor natives to the kingdom of God. He had been badgered by some of the friars in El Paso to let them risk martyrdom in an effort to achieve this goal, but he had been refused every such request.

Fray Ayeta arrived back in El Paso in September 1681. Governor Otermin, who unlike Ayeta had experienced the warriors' fury firsthand, looked with dismay at Ayeta's complement of reluctant colonists and untrained soldiers and pronounced himself most hesitant to undertake a reentry so soon. But Ayeta was a persuasive man, especially when armed with a royal decree, and by early November he and Otermin were marching up the Rio Grande at the head of a new expeditionary force. The force was made up of 146 soldiers and about the same number of Mexican lackeys; a thousand horses, mules, and oxen; and a long line of wagons. No colonists were included; the immediate purpose was to reinvestigate, not to colonize, the land. It had been a year since the Rio Grande Pueblo had been seized by the fever of rebellion, and now the first thing to do was to take their temperature.

The probers' journey up the river took them through a deserted land, past ruined, abandoned villages and devastated fields—until they came to Isleta, which, to their astonishment, was filled with some 1,500 people and was thriving. The people seemed healthy; they said their storage bins were full for the approaching winter. The church was in ruins, but corralled in it were some remnants of colonial livestock. Popé's influence evidently had not yet reached quite this far south.

The villagers announced, with some show of hostility, that they did not want any visitors. The returnees, inspired by Ayeta's missionary fervor, forced their way in, and the villagers decided that they were going to have visitors after all. The leaders approached their guests peacefully and did what they knew was expected of them. They made humble obeisance and sanctimonious noises, pleaded contrition for their sins, begged forgiveness, and asked for readmission to Holy Mother Church. While they were at it, they also requested protection of their stores from raids by less affluent natives to the north. And the visitors, despite the lack of a clear invitation, moved in with their customary self-assurance.

After baptizing the babies born during the past year and destroying masks, ceremonial clothing, prayer sticks, and kachina dolls in a flaming pyre, the visitors sent messengers upriver to the northern villages with promises of pardon and demands for submission. A few days thereafter, having had no reply, Otermin dispatched a captain named Mendoza, with about seventy mounted soldiers, to reconnoiter the north ahead of the main expeditionary force, which Otermin meanwhile would lead more slowly up the river. (This and other aspects of the expedition were to have a very familiar ring.)

It was mid-December now, and frequent blizzards kept the

Mendoza party on the move. Each of the first dozen or so villages was evacuated as he approached, so that he was able, without hindrance, to destroy the usual instruments of the devil and, for punitive good measure, set fire to villagers' stores of winter food. He continued this unamiable policy (on Otermin's orders, of course) until he got as far north as Santo Domingo, where he was confronted by a band of warriors who, after indulging in some hooting and howling and unflattering name-calling, finally calmed down and signaled for a parley. The warrior who came to parley turned out to be none other than Catiti, Popé's loyal assistant. If the inexperienced Mendoza had recognized him, he might have had some second thoughts. But Catiti played his command performance well, begging forgiveness with soulful eyes drenched in perfect contrition and promising to bring other village leaders during the next day or two so that they too could taste the comforts of humiliation. Mendoza and his group settled down in the nearby village of Cochiti and, sure enough, dignified old men began dropping by to take their lumps in a most edifying procession. One of them, however, managed to pass (or let slip) the word to Mendoza that it was all a charade, an elaborate stall designed to give the warriors from the northern villages time to gather and attack. So Mendoza and his troops, after a hasty departure, hurried south to warn Otermin, who was still advancing up the river, destroying deserted villages as he came.

Otermin and Mendoza spent most of the Christmas holiday period quarreling over whether Mendoza and his men had shown the proper spunk in cutting and running. The worsening winter weather was beginning to make everyone else thoroughly miserable when news of a descending rebel horde caused the two leaders to forsake their disputing for the safer course of a quick retreat. On the way past Isleta they discovered that, of the 1,500 repentant inhabitants, 1,115 had repented of the repentance and were already on their way north to join the advancing rebel forces. So Otermin burned the village and, with the 385 stay-at-homes, continued his rapid retreat back to El Paso, arriving there in mid-February

1682. As he had feared in his initial discussion with the ardently evangelical Ayeta, the expedition had turned out to be an utter disaster—except, perhaps, for the psychological effect on people returning to burned-out villages.

Otermin's successor (who shortly was retired in disgrace) was a renowned battle commander named Domingo Jironza Petris Cruzate, whose battle experience was put to several severe tests over the next four years by attacks on El Paso from Apaches and northern Mexicans. These conflicts, together with an extended foray into Texas to forestall French penetration from the east, kept him so busy that he had no time to do more than think vaguely about New Mexico. Then in 1686, after a squabble with the governor of New Biscay, Cruzate was replaced by a man named Reneros, who in 1687 led an invasion of New Mexico, burned a village, and quickly retreated at the first sign of native resistance. He was summarily fired soon thereafter, and Cruzate was reappointed, this time without any responsibility for Texas.

Reneros had been turned back by native resistance at the village of Zia, northwest of present-day Bernalillo, and Cruzate was determined to avenge that defeat and punish the resistance that occasioned it. In the summer of 1688 he led a punitive expedition up the river, stormed the village, killed 600 and captured seventy of its defenders, executed four of its priests in the plaza, and destroyed the town by fire. His appetite thus somewhat satisfied, he returned to El Paso in triumph with his captive villagers, who were promptly added to the slave population.

Meanwhile, Madrid was growing concerned over the delay in reestablishing at least a token colony in New Mexico, and its interest was heightened by new reports of precious metals to be mined—reports no truer than before but no less enticing. The reports only intensified Madrid's interest in reconquering the villages in the Southwest. For this undertaking the viceroy selected an extraordinarily intrepid aristocrat, Don Diego de Vargas Zapata Lujan Ponce de Leon y Contreas.

Vargas's instructions from the viceroy were to bring New

Mexico back under Hispanic control and then to check on those enticing mines (in this case, quicksilver). Not one to be hurried, Vargas decided on two separate but related expeditions, in 1692 and 1693. In 1692 he would conduct an inspection of his province, chiefly to determine how much of it could really be called his. He would take along a force of moderate size and visit the villages of the river people. He would make the usual cross-and-crown demands but would avoid confrontations, at least in general. Many of the villages, he felt sure, would be only too happy to return to the fold. And those that were not too happy would be taken care of by the larger, more forcefully persuasive expedition of 1693. In modern prizefighting parlance, he'd give 'em the ol' one-two.

So Vargas headed north from El Paso in late August 1692 with something less than 200 men: about sixty soldiers and a hundred native fighting men, mostly former Isletans, plus some friars and servants. It was a lonely group as it made its way up the river past empty, crumbling villages and littered, untended farmlands. They saw not a soul, although smoke signals on the hills and in the mountains revealed an unseen presence, probably an Apache presence, all along their route. After about three weeks of this, Vargas called a halt at a deserted hacienda in what today is south Albuquerque, where he set up a kind of fortified headquarters. Here he left about half of his invasion force, with most of the supplies, and continued north himself with about forty soldiers and fifty of the Isleta warriors. Not a village along the river was inhabited, not even Cochiti or Santo Domingo. Only when the intruders reached the top of a hill overlooking Santa Fe did they see signs of human occupation. Here natives from east of the river, driven west by hunger and Apache raids, had built a native village amid the ruins of the old capital. Apparently the town was a rather pathetic sight, constructed in haste.

Vargas ordered his troops to approach the town before morning light, but no one was to behave in a belligerent or menacing way. Once they were in front of the town, he would give a signal, and they could shout, "Glory to the blessed sacrament of the altar!"—a pious and inspirational selection

An early engraving of Don Diego de Vargas

from their repertory of organized hubbub, one perhaps as menacing to the residents as anything else might have been at that point. If and when the company was to attack, he would give the signal by drawing his sword. He hoped that this would not be necessary. For Vargas, violence would be a last resort. He wanted this to be a bloodless reconquest as far as possible, and it would be perfectly possible if he encountered no resistance.

And so it was that the occupants of Santa Fe were awakened by the strains of blood-circulating hullabaloo before dawn that morning. Warriors rushed up to the roof of the old governor's palace and peered out into the dark, trying to identify the source of the peculiar commotion. Vargas instructed one of his Isletans to announce that the Hispanics had returned to forgive the natives their transgressions and to restore the rule of the two majesties. The warriors on the palace roof expressed some doubt: if these were the same kind of pale-faced visitors, why weren't they firing guns? No firing of guns, Vargas replied, but when the sun was up they would see the Blessed Virgin on his flag. (Mary had been drafted as the spiritual protector for this invasion, and Vargas had brought a statue of her along. It is honored today in the Santa Fe cathedral, under the name of "La Conquistadora.")

If Vargas expected this appeal to the Blessed Virgin to hasten the capitulation, he was disappointed. He did not have to wait for the dawn. One of the Isletan warriors suggested that he sound a trumpet, and he responded not only by having a military trumpet blown but also by ordering a long drum roll as accompaniment. This musical assault instantly convinced the Santa Feans, who spent the next hour building up their courage with war dances and other displays of loud defiance. Vargas positioned his troops as though for attack and, daylight having come, ordered some men to start on a very conspicuous interruption of the town's water supply. Then once again he called for surrender.

Some of the Santa Fe warriors answered with a demand that he come forward and show himself. Probably to their surprise, he did just that, despite the drawn bows of warriors on the palace roof. Riding forward and taking off his helmet, he displayed a calm courage that even his most implacable enemy could respect. He offered them, he said, the king's pardon, and the friars would bring them God's pardon. All very well, one of the warriors retorted, but if the villagers surrendered they once again would be forced to spend all their time working for the colonists, building churches and haciendas, tilling their fields and tending their orchards—or they would be mercilessly whipped. He mentioned three colonial officials noted for their cruel treatment of natives in the days of misery. Vargas tried to reassure him: neither those three nor any like them were with *this* expedition. And now the besiegers would give the defenders an hour to consider their proposition.

He turned and went back to his tent for breakfast. (It consisted of some biscuits and hot chocolate. Drinking hot chocolate had become quite the fashion in Europe since Coronado's time, and Vargas seems to have been addicted to the hot-chocolate break.) He also ordered that the preparations for siege and assault be continued, including the ostentatious positioning of his two bronze cannons. Before the hour was up, an armed warrior strode out of the town and approached the aggressors' camp. Vargas, emerging from his tent as the man came up to it, stretched out his hand in a gesture of friendship. Ignoring it, the man said that he had come to take two of the friars back with him into the town. Although several friars immediately volunteered, Vargas counseled caution and restraint. He had heard an alarm signal from some of the guards posted on the other side of town, and he felt that an investigation was in order. The warrior returned to the town without his friars.

The alarm had been sounded because groups of warriors from other villages had appeared at the top of a nearby hill. There was no attack, however; instead, one of the chiefs came to Vargas to parley. The governor's courtesy so won him over that he went into the town and argued for surrender. The expedition, he explained, had returned only to restore the fallen-away Pueblos to a state of grace, politically and spiritually. They had not come to punish anyone. He may have meant this sincerely; but the villages were anything but united in friendship, and he may have had an ulterior motive. The Santa Fe warriors, at any rate, would have none of it. Rejecting his overtures as humbug, they asserted their willingness to die rather than surrender, adding that he should feel free to leave at once and rejoin their enemies. He did so, crestfallen.

Their firm resolve weakened, however, as they watched the besiegers deliberately preparing for a heavy assault—checking their muskets, loading the cannon, packing sacks of gunpowder against the garrison's walls. The fact that this was being done by unprotected soldiers in full view of the defenders was particularly unnerving. It must have crossed the warriors' minds that this might be only the advance party of an overwhelming force which could appear at any moment. They sent Vargas a message: if he would remove the soldiers and the cannons, as well as disarm himself, they would come out and parley with him. Vargas refused. He had not issued any ultimatum, he answered, nor had he explicitly threatened the town. The soldiers and the cannons would stay put. The defenders would have to accept this word as a Christian that they would not be harmed.

This promise was not as soothing as Vargas may have expected. The warriors had painful memories of former Christian guarantees. But, after some more dickering, a warrior came out of the town, matching Vargas's courage in being unarmed. The governor dismounted, greeted him most amiably, and stood there with him for some time in friendly conversation. Before long two more warriors emerged and were given the same warm greeting. The friars, sensing an opportunity, begged Vargas for permission to enter the town. (Theoretically at least, like the Moors who had so strongly influenced Spanish thinking, they considered a violent death in God's service as an instant release into paradise.) The governor agreed, and two of the friars entered the town alone and, of course, unarmed. However the villagers may have interpreted this, they soon were flocking around the two missionaries, begging for peace and forgiveness and receiving their blessings.

Dusk was approaching. At this point most if not all of Vargas's predecessors would almost certainly have led their troops into the town, helped themselves to food and other supplies, and settled in for the night. But Vargas was cool and perceptive as well as brave. He suspected that the people in town must still be divided, with at least a strong minority in favor of resistance. So he elected to spend the night, at least, outside the town, thus giving the town's right-thinking element a chance to win over the recalcitrant. He ordered the bulk of his forces to fall back and make camp some distance from the town and then—after a final word to the defenders, to the effect that they could show their goodwill next morning by erecting a cross in front of the palace and wearing small crosses on their breasts—he followed. He must have been nervous about those friars, but, as he reported later, he had "decided to put some trust in destiny."

The next morning, dressed not as a soldier but as a royal courtier, he returned to the plain outside the town with his captains and some soldiers. A large group of warriors met him there, peaceably, and invited him to come into the town with the Franciscan superior-general and half a dozen soldiers without their guns. Mass could be celebrated, they promised, in the governor's palace. Over his captains' strenuous objections, Vargas and the friar agreed, and the little group disappeared into the town with the warriors, the gate closing behind them with an unsettling finality.

Vargas probably anticipated that the villagers were looking for a display of cool courage, and he had no intention of disappointing them. Inside the town he found himself and his party surrounded by armed warriors ranged all along the roofs. Come down from there, he demanded, and leave your weapons behind. Doubtless to the visitors' considerable relief, they did so. And then a welcome sight greeted the guests as they turned a corner: a large cross was standing in the plaza, in front of the palace—"a beautiful cross," as the expeditioner's chronicler described it. Vargas ran through the usual formal rigmarole, relaying the royal pardon on condition of acceptable contrition and once again taking possession of absolutely everything and everybody in the name of His Most Catholic Majesty. Amid loud huzzahs and hymn singing, the villagers were led in cheering "Long live the king!" For them, even after a century and a half of this sort of thing, it must have been like swearing allegiance to the Man in the Moon.

The next morning, during a solemn mass, the children born during the Christian absence, about a thousand of them, were baptized. Many of the babies, unlike their elders, protested vociferously. Meanwhile, the chiefs of several nearby villages evidently gathered together and concluded that their wisest course would be to pay Vargas a visit in Santa Fe and offer their submission and cooperation. During the next week or so they filed in and performed the required obeisance. Among them was Tupatu, Popé's old lieutenant, who offered the governor his help in subduing Pecos, which apparently had shown a spirit of independence that he resented. He had brought along some 300 armed men as a token of his sincerity. Vargas invited him to enjoy a hot-chocolate break with him.

While still in El Paso, the governor had been promised fifty soldiers by the governor of New Biscay, and he had been awaiting their arrival ever since. Partly because they still had not come—it was now mid-September—he accepted Tupatu's offer, although he stipulated that he wanted to avoid violence whenever possible and was not about to go into the business of punishing repentant villagers for resistance to Tupatu, or indeed for any other reason. The belligerent chief accepted this proviso, perhaps because he didn't believe a word of it. If he had known about leopards, he would also have had an opinion about spots. But he was in for some surprises.

About halfway to Pecos, Vargas was astonished by the arrival of the 50 soldiers from New Biscay, which brought the strength of his entire party to nearly 500 fighting men. This was more than enough, he felt, to convert even a village the size of Pecos without firing a shot. But when they arrived at Pecos on September 23, the village proved a serious disappointment. Its inhabitants had fled into the nearby mountains, and the town was deserted. Vargas dispatched a few squads into the mountains, and before long they came back with a couple of dozen captives. Treating them humanely, Vargas sent some of them back into the mountains with an invitation to their fellow refugees to return in peace. In this case, however,

Remains of the Mission San José de Laguna at Laguna Pueblo (A)
and its extraordinary interior murals (B).

the results were a further disappointment. He could not overcome the flood of bitter memories that the return of the foreigners must have evoked. The people stayed in hiding, and not even the messengers returned. After four or five days of waiting, he ordered preparations for continuing the expedition into the northern river country. He released the rest of the captives unharmed and, over the heated objections of some captains with a greater reverence for soldierly custom, left without destroying even a part of the village.

This act of unprecedented restraint undoubtedly served him well during the rest of his extended tour. It must have deeply impressed Tupatu, who was largely responsible for the welcome that the visitors received during their visits to the northern river villages. They were greeted everywhere by villagers holding up small crosses as symbols of their contrition and eagerness to be taken back into the fold. Dances were held in the visitors' honor, and the baptism business flourished mightily. Vargas's reputation for relative magnaminity clearly had diminished the natives' hostility. More important, his reputation for almost superhuman courage (of which he was to give further evidence) was developing into a mystique. Cooperation with this charismatic man, especially when he seemed to want nothing more than ritualistic expressions of submissions, obviously was an easier and safer course than resistance.

Nevertheless, at Taos, the northernmost village, Vargas was informed that the leaders of several other villages were planning to ambush his party as an initial step in ridding the land of foreigners once again. As it turned out, this report probably was false. But if his informants hoped that the news would cause him to leave hurriedly for the south, they were not disappointed. He left immediately for Santa Fe, where he could refurbish his troops and prepare for any show of rebellion.

While there, he wrote the viceroy a detailed report of his success in reestablishing the faith among Pueblos. He added, however, that this reestablishment would prove highly impermanent without a strong Christian presence in the territory; he had not been entirely taken in by the native show of affec-

tion. He urged the viceroy to consider sending at least 500 settlers into New Mexico, with at least 100 soldiers to garrison
the capital of Santa Fe, since the natives' Christianity, without
a military force to keep the lid on, would soon evaporate.

Vargas's stay in Santa Fe was brief. It was now mid-
October, and he knew what bitter weather winter could bring
to the high desert country. With some sixty horsemen he rode
to Pecos, prepared for a full military assault. About a mile outside the town some four or five hundred warriors confronted
him. At his command the soldiers formed a wedge, with the
governor at its tip, and prepared to attack. The warriors had
come out, however, not to fight but to parley. Reassured that
he did not intend either to destroy or to occupy their village—
the mystique must have been at work, for they surely would
not have been willing to take the word of any other
European—they led him into the town peacefully for what had
now become a routine ceremony of reconciliation.

Encouraged by this turn of events (since Pecos had been
one of the villages reportedly in a state of rebellion), Vargas
turned back west, paying calls on the villages southwest of
Santa Fe and receiving the subservient welcomes that he had
by now come largely to expect. Even at Zia, which Cruzate
had so brutally sacked four years earlier, he was received at a
dilapidated encampment in the hills some miles from the village. Lacking tools, the disheartened survivors had never
rebuilt it. When Vargas promised them some tools, the villagers celebrated with a dance. And the governor continued
on his way.

At the village of Jemez the initial greeting was not so
friendly. As the expedition approached, a band of warriors
swept down on them from a nearby hill. The attack was a
curious one, however. Instead of using their weapons, the
warriors threw dust into the soldiers eyes. Unflinching, Vargas
passed along an order that no one was to retaliate, on penalty
of death. As the cavalrymen trotted steadily on through the
dust clouds, the warriors lost heart, fell back, and permitted
the intruders to enter the village. Although the welcome was

a cold one, the mystique was at work, and the submission ritual was performed without incident, if also without warmth.

Vargas now headed for his hacienda headquarters at the site of Albuquerque. On the way he stopped at Santo Domingo. Here, too, the welcome was cold, but there was no resistance, probably in part because the travelers were still accompanied by Tupatu, with his considerable influence, and his warriors. But at the hacienda headquarters the chief announced that his men were already late for the harvesting at home; he and his warriors would have to return to their villages, leaving no more than thirty men to go with Vargas on his expedition to the western villages. Vargas, disappointed but sympathetic, agreed.

Over the objections of some of his captains, who wanted to postpone the western tour and return to El Paso for the winter, the governor chose about ninety soldiers and, with the thirty lucky Tupatuans, headed west for Acoma. Arriving there early in November, he was met by a large band of warriors who, looking down on the expedition from the edge of their high cliff, strongly advised them to keep right on going. Vargas called up to them to surrender, offering them the usual king's pardon, but his charisma may have been somewhat diffused over the intervening several hundred feet. The warriors replied that, if he continued on his western journey now, he might find them more amenable on his return trip. Vargas simply ordered his men to set up camp for the night.

The next morning, like Vincente de Zaldivar before him, he did what the villagers must have considered physically impossible. With nine picked men, he climbed the cliff and appeared quite unexpectedly in the village. Unlike Zaldivar, however, he did not attack, and in utter consternation the villagers submitted. And then, after the customary rituals and baptisms, the visitors departed in peace. The villagers watched them with what must have been glazed eyes.

The Zunis proved surprisingly well prepared for the governor's visit. Not only did they welcome him warmly and submit peaceably, but they also showed him something which they knew would please him. They took him to a small room containing a number of Christian artifacts—a statue of Jesus and a picture of St. John the Baptist, with a couple of holy candles burning before them. There even were some books on Christian subjects, left behind by a martyred friar—killed, the guides hastened to add, at another village. Vargas was deeply touched by this unique display of Christian durability. He thanked the villagers, assuring them of a special place in his affections from that day forward.

In Hopi territory he met with some resistance, but cool courage and restraint won yet another day. It was now mid-November, and the idea of returning to El Paso—several hundred miles to the south and several thousand feet lower in elevation—was rapidly gaining great popularity. After obtaining some unpromising samples of ore from the fabled quicksilver mines in the area, Vargas turned and hurried homeward. The return trip took almost a month, despite a shortcut. It was a miserable month, for the men were cold and thirsty and thoroughly exhausted, the last partly from having to fend off several Apache attacks. But on December 20 they finally got back to El Paso, where, needless to say, they found the welcome they received the most gratifying of all.

They had been gone, incredibly, only four months. They had reconquered New Mexico without losing a single man, without killing a single villager. Over 2,000 young natives had been baptized. The Pueblos had been restored to the rule of cross and crown merely by bloodless intimidation. It was an astounding achievement.

Its effects, however, proved even more fleeting than Vargas had expected. As soon as the proselytizers were gone, the villages reverted to their own religion, with perhaps three or four exceptions. (Without a written record, of course, we can't be sure of details; the exceptions, though unlikely, are mentioned here as possibilities, inferred from later Hispanic reports.) Religious persecution classically feeds the thing it preys on. The dedication of the Pueblos to their ancient religion was kept alive not only by the chief priests and "healers," who obviously had a vested interest in its survival, but also by the hard-sell aspects of the invaders' missionary technique. Whatever its faults, the native religion was more down-to-earth, literally as well as figuratively. For centuries it had governed their gentle relationship with nature, their ceremonies, their fun, their daily lives, their minds and hearts. It was not a thing to be easily abandoned.

In October 1693, Vargas returned to complete his reconquest and was dismayed to find that he virtually would have to start all over again. It had taken him nine months to gather another expeditionary force, and about 400 native warriors and servants who had been persuasively volunteered from refugee camps clustered about El Paso. It also included eighteen supply wagons, 2,000 horses, 1,000 mules, and 900 head of cattle. Unlike the expedition of 1692, this was designed for more than a tentative, preliminary investigation.

On his trip upriver Vargas did not stop to investigate deserted villages along the way, but he did send a messenger ahead to inform the villagers of his reinvasion and to remind them of their oaths of fealty. The messenger returned with word that the natives were preparing themselves for resistance. Only three or four villages, southeast and southwest of Santa Fe, were ready if not eager to receive him peaceably; Santa Ana, San Felipe, and Pecos; Zia apparently was on the fence but leaning in the right direction. By December 16, when the expedition reached Santa Fe, it was clear to Vargas that this time the villagers might not be so easy to push around.

The inhabitants of Santa Fe greeted him coldly but without any threats of violence. They even gave him some corn, though not as much as he requested. He told them that they would have to evacuate the town, explaining that it was not their village but had been founded by the colonists. The villagers, doubtless remembering how they happened to be there, as well as who had actually built the town, simply ignored his demand with an unconcern that he must have found intensely irritating.

But with characteristic restraint, he decided to give them some time to think it over. The intruders set up camp outside the town and braced themselves for the rigors of the chilling winter nights. They had already lost thirty women and children to the rigors of the march from El Paso, and during the next few nights they were to lose another twenty-two children to the bitter cold. One can imagine the pressure on Vargas to end the suffering by attacking the town and throwing the villagers out.

He held on to his hope for almost two weeks, but the villagers, far from relenting, further expressed their intransigence by refusing to give the intruders any more corn. On December 28 the governor issued an ultimatum: leave at once or be evicted. It was ignored. On the next day, he threw his full military force, augmented by 140 warriors newly arrived from Pecos, into an assault on the town. The results were what most Christians and at least many natives had come to expect: defeat and heavy casualties on the villagers' side, victory and extremely light casualties on the other. The next morning, after their chief had committed suicide, the villagers surrendered, and Vargas summarily executed seventy of their leaders. And so the message went out: no more nice guy. He had no intention of finishing last.

Shortly before the attack, a request for some missionaries had come down from a few of the villages to the north. There were eighteen friars with the expedition, but none displayed the zeal for martyrdom that some of their predecessors had shown in the past. The resistance at Santa Fe had rather unnerved them, and the execution of seventy natives was not likely to ensure their continued good health beyond the walls of the capital. They petitioned Vargas not to send them north alone and unprotected, and the governor, now more than ever convinced that only soldiers could really convert the people of the Rio Grande, allowed them to stay.

The colonial community of Santa Fe had now been reestablished, but, ironically, it was dependent for sustenance on the Pueblos. Vargas dispatched several raiding parties to various villages to requisition food supplies, but to a great extent the harassed residents foiled him by destroying their supplies before the raiders could get to them. Rumors were growing of another revolt in the offing. Vargas determined to forestall it by going on the offensive. Clearly he felt that he hadn't already been offensive enough. The message had been transmitted, but had it been received?

Early in January 1694, a band of warriors had gathered near the village of San Ildefonso, and Vargas had taken some men and accosted the warriors with a demand for surrender. In reply, they had suggested that he and a friar come alone into their camp, as he had done occasionally in 1692, but, with an eye on the change in climate, he decided not to take the risk. After estimating the balance of local military power, he had retreated to Santa Fe. Now, in early March, he set out with a larger force to teach the hostiles a lesson. The warriors, however, had increased their numbers and improved their defenses, and they were not in a receptive mood for a lesson. After a five-hour battle and thirty-five Hispanic casualties, Vargas withdrew and sent back to Santa Fe for reinforcements. They arrived on March 11, and for eight days Vargas repeatedly stormed the warriors' encampment. But this time he was defeated, his efforts frustrated by the terrain (the encampment was on a mesa), the weather, and the warriors' grim defiance. He managed to capture a supply of food, but otherwise the extended sortie had been nothing more than a further provocation. He and his men limped back to Santa Fe.

In mid-April he made up for this defeat in an attack on a mesa near the village of Cochiti. His success consisted of hundreds of dead and wounded warriors, captured women and children, a large supply of corn and livestock, and destruction of a village. To his warrior allies he allotted 200 head of cattle in gratitude for their assistance, and doubtless in an attempt to sharpen the division of native opinion on the relative merits of resistance and cooperation. That division already was serious. In May, for instance, a band of native collaborators attacked the village of Jemez on their own initiative, but were driven off.

The growing native disenchantment with the practicality of resistance, aggravated by intertribal hostilities, was to serve Vargas well over the next several months. With the help of warriors from "friendly" villages, he subdued Taos in June,

Jemez in July, and San Ildefonso in September. These battles quenched the flames of active rebellion. During the last three months of 1694 he tried to dispel at least some of the hatred that had fed those flames, offering villages what help he could to get them through the winter. He reinstituted the system of village governors appointed by Santa Fe, thus reassuring the administrative authority of the crown. Friars were once again assigned to the villages, reasserting the spiritual authority of the cross, or at least of the papal tiara. But more important than anything Vargas did do was what he did not do: he did not reinstitute the despised encomienda system, and he did not require that Christianity replace the native religion. From this point on, Native Americans could not be forced to cultivate only the fields of others or to worship only the gods of others. These two conditions which, more than anything else, had brought on the revolt of 1680, would now largely disappear. Vargas, thorough man that he was, must have carefully read the report of the commission that investigated that revolt.

Revolution simmered under the surface during the rest of the seventeenth century, boiling up only once, in June 1696. Serious yet limited in scope, this rebellion kept Vargas very busy for several months putting out fires (or, in another sense, starting them). By the end of the year, he had managed to suppress the rebellion with the usual methods. For the last time, the restless natives subsided, settling into a kind of arm's-length harmony with the colonists. The relationship was, and is today, at best an uneasy symbiosis.

For Vargas the rest of the century was a nightmare having nothing to do with the villagers. In 1697 his replacement as governor, a man named Cubero, arrived from Mexico City. Cubero reportedly was self-indulgent, vindictive, emotionally unstable, and mindlessly sadistic, among other things. Vargas's enemies, seeing an opportunity before them, brought charges against him. Cubero listened, and he too saw an opportunity; the footprints of such men often grace the backs of their betters. As a result, the last of the conquistadors spent the next three years incommunicado in a jail cell at one end of the governor's palace. In 1700 a sympathetic friar reported his plight to an astonished viceroy, who ordered that Vargas be brought to Mexico City at once. Before long he was governor of New Mexico again, as well as a marquis by royal command (he had always wanted some such title). Vargas returned to Santa Fe in 1703, where he died in 1704. Cubero simply disappeared.

The reconquest was complete now, and the task of colonizing began in earnest. During the eighteenth century, Hispanic haciendas and other settlements grew up all along the Rio Grande, including towns like Santa Cruz and Albuquerque. The colonial population rose from about 1,500 to about 20,000. The survivors among the people of the Rio Grande, saddled with friars and governors but now otherwise largely unmolested, settled down in a spirit of resignation. For them it was a miserable century. Their population, already so severely depleted by conquest during the two preceding centuries, dwindled further under the introduction of European diseases such as measles and smallpox, until it was less than half of what it had been 200 years before. For the survivors, the reinstated Juans and Marias, the struggle for religious and civil and personal freedom was over. Portions of their culture would continue to exist, but only through supervisory tolerance or oversight. Some change would come, but not for many decades, and even then it would not, it could not, restore a past lost in the mists of memory.

CHAPTER FIVE
ANGLO POLICY AND PUEBLO RECOVERY

The Indian problem as it exists today, including the heaviest and most unproductive administration costs of public service, has largely grown out of the allotment system which has destroyed the economic integrity of the Indian estate and deprived the Indians of normal economic and human activity.

EXTRACT FROM THE ANNUAL REPORT OF THE COMMISSIONER OF INDIAN AFFAIRS JOHN COLLIER, 1934

THE WORST WAS OVER for the native populations along the Rio Grande, although the best would never be recovered. The river territory was no longer theirs, but neither had it been entirely taken from them. The invaders had given some of the land back in the form of royal land grants. These grants, subsequently recognized by Mexico and then the United States of America, were to give them considerable legal protection over the next century from the kind of wholesale land-grabbing that would dispossess so many other Native Americans.

Their lives would be radically affected by two changes that

occurred during the eighteenth century on another continent some 6,000 miles away: the decline of Spain, in favor of an ascendant France; and the Enlightenment, which loosened the absolutist grip of preordained oligarchy and introduced a respect for human dignity and equality into social and political operations not only in the Old World but in the New World as well. The decline of Spanish wealth and military power had its reverberations along the Rio Grande, where the settlers were kept much too busy fending off, and recovering from, Navajo and Apache raids. In 1822 Spanish power disappeared completely from the territory, which now came under the jurisdiction of a newly independent Mexico too deeply preoccupied with its own problems to make its presence felt north of El Paso. The territory was virtually cast adrift. It was a power vacuum, with a power right next door very eager to fill it. In 1846, by the Treaty of Guadalupe Hidalgo, New Mexico became a territory of the United States. The United States government, under the treaty, became responsible for protecting the pueblos along the Rio Grande and their land grants from all aggressors, whether Navajos, Apaches, Hispanos or Anglos.

The U.S. Cavalry's powers of persuasion were considerable. The raiding began tapering off immediately, and within a generation it ceased altogether. Indeed, the principal violence in 1847 seems to have been furnished by a rebel group of Indians and Hispanos from Taos, who killed and scalped the U.S. governor in an otherwise abortive and very local revolt, the last in which any of the Rio Grande Pueblos were ever to be involved. Despite this unpleasant episode (which may have arisen from a misunderstanding of Anglo intentions), the government of the new territory drew a long overdue distinction between the quiet, inoffensive Rio Grande Pueblos and the fierce raiders of the plains. In that same year the territorial legislature formally confirmed each village's right to its land grant, in perpetuity, and its existence as a recognized unit of local government.

In 1849 a Federal agency office was established at Santa Fe

with jurisdiction over San Juan Pueblos as well as over the raiders of the plains. Its job was to protect the former and pacify the later. Under the program, which the Federal agency initiated, San Juan Pueblos were given small-arms weapons for defense, with the understanding that they would not take the offensive—no retaliatory raids, no preemptive strikes. Each village would receive technical assistance, Peace Corps style, mostly in the form of a resident blacksmith and a government agent with some agricultural expertise. And the people would be educated in the political ways of their new masters through a program in which village leaders would be brought to Washington, D.C., for an inspirational visit and then return to spread the gospel of democracy. That democracy did not, however, include anything in the way of participation among the Pueblos.

The plan was slow to get started and was never fully implemented. The federal authorities were preoccupied with other matters, especially over the next three or four decades. It took about that long to subdue the unruly hostiles of the plains and to confine them to reservations. And then there was the Civil War, in which the boys from Dixie gave a right smart account of themselves in New Mexico, reaching Santa Fe before turning back. Finally, there was the invasion of the Anglos.

During the 1880s, adventurers, pioneers, and settlers swarmed into New Mexico from the increasingly citified east. Although this invasion, quite unlike earlier ones, involved virtually no direct contact with the pueblos, it threatened to be even more devastating. As the Anglos spread out over the territory, buying it up, homesteading it, or simply squatting on it, they exerted increasing pressure on the Hispanos—earlier settlers who were now considered third-class citizens in the area. The Anglos pushed the Hispanos, who in turn pushed, or rather compressed, Native Americans, who in turn watched apprehensively as their farm and ranch lands were whittled down, slice by precious slice.

The pueblos of the Rio Grande were particularly vulner-

Photograph taken by Edward S. Curtis
at the Zuni Pueblo, 1903

able because of the Supreme Court decision of 1876, which ruled that their land was not reservation land but rather private property, to which they held title under the old royal land grants. As a result, because their land was not "reserved" for them by treaties with the United States, the Federal government had no obligation to protect it from encroachment even with court injunctions, much less with guns. Furthermore, the Court said that the U.S. government had no legal obligation to render assistance of any kind to Pueblos, and thus no right to spend public money on them. By 1913, when a subsequent Court of a different persuasion reversed this ruling, Pueblos were almost outnumbered by trespassers on their land. Taos lost much of its land to the adjacent settlement town of Taos; Santa Clara lost much to Espanola. Every village was similarly dispossessed. The only exceptions were Acoma and Zia, presumably because of their locations.

The 1913 decision came none too soon. Suits brought by the Pueblo communities in New Mexico had consistently been exercises in futility: either the decisions went against Native Americans, or they were denied the right to bring suit in the first place. With the immigrant population burgeoning—from 100,000 in 1910 to 360,000 in 1920—each pueblo might have wound up with about an acre apiece if it had not been for the Supreme Court's reversal of its 1876 ruling. That judicial support of the villagers' cause, however, spurred some of the greedier trespassers to seek legislative relief at the federal level, and in 1922 the U.S. Congress almost passed a bill that would have legalized the "trespass quo." A major reason for its defeat was the organization of an All-Pueblo Council, the villages' first show of unity since the revolt of 1680. With the help of sympathetic settlers, the Council was instrumental not only in the defeat of this legislation but also in the passage of the Pueblo Lands Act in 1924, which restored all royal-grant lands to the villages, or compensation in those cases in which restoration was no longer legally possible. The Pueblos were learning to play by the Anglo rules of the game.

Another effect of the Anglo invasion was somewhat more

remote but none the less terrifying. Unlike Pueblos, Anglos generally considered nature as something to exploit rather than cooperate with. During the last third of the nineteenth century, they enterprisingly denuded the plains with overgrazing and much of the nearby mountainsides with their logging operations, turning the blessings of snow and rain into torrential disasters. All along the Rio Grande and the rivers that fed it, centuries-old farms succumbed to floodwaters. Between the 1880s and the 1930s, when the New Deal began accelerating federal programs in flood control and soil conservation, almost every village lost land to the new procedures. To this day, neither the land nor the balance of nature has been restored, although the losses have been at least partly compensated for by the government's introduction of new agricultural techniques—synthetic fertilizers, mechanical threshing, and harvesting—to increase the yield of the remaining land.

Like their predecessors, the Anglo authorities were instinctively dedicated to the principle of acculturation: the river people would have to be converted from the miseries of an obviously inferior culture to the joys of an obviously superior one. The most promising method of conversion, Anglos believed, was education. In other words, "as the sapling is bent, so grows the tree." In the 1880s the government began a program of running boarding schools so that children could be freed from the aboriginal influence of their parents and educated in such things as masonry and carpentry for boys, sewing and cooking for girls, and modern civilized values for all. By 1922 about eighty-five percent of the native children were enrolled, in effect, in foreign schools—thirty-eight percent in government boarding schools, twenty-two percent in Catholic boarding schools, and twenty-five percent in thirteen day schools in or near some of the villages—schools in which they generally were taught English, for instance, not as a foreign language but as though they had been born to it, or should have been.

For a while in the 1920s, the children were not allowed to

go back to their villages to take part in native religious ceremonies. During this period, the Bureau of Indian Affairs tried to apply its Religious Crimes Code to the river people. It clucked officially over the initiation ceremonies at Taos, for instance, which its report described as depraved rituals conducted by "half-animals." This monitoring program was not widely supported outside the Bureau, however, and eventually it died for lack of nourishment.

Pueblos generally tried to keep to themselves, minding their own business as best they could, as had been their practice for centuries. Unfortunately this very effort, in the face of persistent external pressure to rectify their spiritual condition, created dissension in the villages or aggravated it where it already existed. In Laguna, in the 1870s and 1880s, a couple of vigorous Presbyterian missionaries, Walter and Robert Marmon, developed a following among the villagers. Their influence was considerable: Walter married the daughter of one of the village leaders, and in 1879 Robert was made governor. Their devotion to the segregation of the saved from the unsaved split the village into hostile factions. Feelings ran so high that finally some of the "conservatives" (those dedicated to maintaining the old-time religion) packed up their things and left to establish a separate community near Isleta.

Religious differences also created problems at Taos. A child who had been sent to boarding school came back a man with a strong devotion to the Native American Church—a religion begun in 1890, formally incorporated in 1918, and based on a belief in the sacramental character of peyote, a stimulant drug derived from parts of a cactus plant. He established a branch of the church in the village, gained a few adherents, and conducted meetings bathed in drug-induced euphoria. Although his church never made headway against the old religion—which even his followers did not completely desert—it managed to cause some violent altercations and to persist as a source of trouble.

In Isleta the factionalism was political rather than religious, arising out of the Bureau's efforts to convert the pueblos to a constitutional, U.S.-style form of local government. At San Ildefonso the controversy was over the location of the main plaza, with the inhabitants splitting into north-plaza and south-plaza parties. There also was trouble over the growing independence of women in the tribe. Throughout the river communities, new controversies arose, and old controversies were exacerbated by the strains of living in the midst of meddling conquerors.

The economic changes among Pueblos were considerable. With their land boundaries defined and protected by the Pueblo Lands Act of 1924, and even extended by purchase with compensation money, the people were more secure in terms of real property than they had been even before the arrival of Coronado. Partly because of this new security, their population began to increase, and some of their young people began declaring a measure of independence by seeking work outside the villages, on the railroad and in the ever-expanding Hispano-Anglo towns. This infused the villages not only with supplementary income but also with new and controversial ideas about cultural values.

Around the turn of the century, another source of income for many of the villages began to slowly develop: Pueblo art and crafts. It started with pottery. This was a craft that had suffered a decline with the introduction of metal and ceramic pots and pans, but now the new transcontinental railway was bringing affluent tourists and eager anthropologists to the river valley and interest in southwestern archaeology and crafts. Led by the virtuosity of the celebrated potter Maria Montoya Martinez of San Ildefonso, and later assisted by a government agency called the Indian Arts and Crafts Board, the villages turned out

Women at a water hole near the Acoma pueblo are wearing silverwork and jewelry and carrying handcrafted pottery—popular tourist items at the turn of the century.

beautifully crafted pots by the thousands. Baskets, too, became quite popular with collectors, as did turquoise jewelry, blankets, silver and leather work, and even kachina dolls. Even in competition with the cheaper, machine-made imitations that flooded the market, their crafts at least contributed to their economic welfare, even if it was only a matter of rising from a level of destitution to one of genteel poverty.

Some of the villages experienced a suburban exodus of sorts. Residents who preferred more open living than what the relatively crowded villages provided began to recognize that, with the elimination of Apache and Navajo raids, it was now safe to live outside the village, closer to the fields. This became an important consideration especially during planting and harvesting times. At first only makeshift shelters were built during those times, but soon houses, usually built with federal help, began appearing around the villages. In some cases, the cluster housing overshadowed the villages themselves in area and population. Like the Anglos in the well-packed cities of the East, the Pueblo were developing a taste for open space, easier living, and the comforts of privacy. The villages, however, generally maintained their religious and political identity. The plazas still were used for dancing and singing and other forms of public prayer, and the kivas were still the centers of authority. The village churches and their missionaries still were predominantly Catholic, although Jesuit priests and secular clergy replaced Franciscan friars. Each village had its own way of accommodating the ancient religion to the demands of Christianity. In some of the villages the distinction was kept fairly sharp, but in most there was a good deal of blending. It proved quite easy, for instance, to associate the Pueblos' "Woman Who Thinks" with the Catholics' "Mary, Mother of God."

Christians have never really understood the accommodation, because the Pueblo have managed to protect their traditional religion with a veil of secrecy, operating on the principle that the less foreigners know, the better. That veil has been penetrated somewhat, of course, chiefly by anthropologists and interested government agents, who on occasion have not been above bribing a susceptible villager to reveal a secret or two. In general, however, the reaction of the people to outsiders' efforts at penetrating their carefully guarded traditions have been to increase the guards. The abortive but zealous religious purge of the seventeenth century had been a memorably traumatic experience for them, as was the Bureau's twentieth-century abortive attempt to apply its Religious Crimes Code to the more uninhibited of their ceremonies. Largely as a result, in recent years the veil has, if anything, grown stronger and more opaque.

In the 1920s, the pueblos also had to contend with some political missionary pressure from the Bureau to remodel their form of local government in the likeness of U.S. representative democracy—with each village adopting a written constitution, universal suffrage, and so on. The pressure, however, was much gentler than that exerted in earlier times for religious remodeling, and only five or six pueblos made any substantial changes. Nevertheless, the pressure had some effect. By introducing new ideas, it contributed to the gradual erosion of native culture. In this respect, of course, ideas have been much more effective than guns.

But the guns were there, like a headmaster's cane in the corner. The United States' conquest of the Pueblos has been contrasted with the Spanish conquest, although it is not always quite fair to make this comparison. It clearly was accompanied by less bloodshed. Yet we must remember that the villagers were already a defeated, exhausted people when the Anglos took over. Further, they could understand that the U.S. Army, unlike the conquistadors, had no critical logistic problems, and they could observe, almost firsthand, the brutal efficiency with which U.S. troops subdued other Native Americans. Resistance obviously would have been suicidal, so they chose an alternative—surrender—and opted for dignified accommodation. And that substantially is the situation as it exists today.

In 1913, when the U.S. Supreme Court reversed itself and

recognized the Pueblos as "Indians" legally entitled to federal protection and funding, the decision described them as
"essentially a simple, uninformed and inferior people." If this
disdainful characterization typified some of the most exalted
legal minds in the country, one can imagine how tightly prej-
udice has gripped less celebrated minds among the Pueblos'
Anglo neighbors and among bureaucrats appointed to deal
with their inferiority. When Congress granted all Native
Americans full U.S. citizenship in 1924, the new law was more
imaginative than descriptive. Today, half a century later, it is
far from fully realized.

Though the Pueblo population nearly tripled between
1900 and 1970 (to about 30,000), it dwindled rapidly in proportion to New Mexico's total population. In 1970 Anglos
outnumbered them twenty to one, and Hispanos outnumbered them by seven to one. Their own growth in population
has severely strained village resources, forcing many of the
younger people to work for minimum wages in nearby towns.
This supplementary income has not quite raised the people to
dizzying heights of affluence: the average family income is
estimated at something less than $1,000 a year, and they have
twice as many families on welfare, proportionally, as the rest
of the state's population. Their unemployment rate is regularly double that of the country at large; only about a third of
their employable people are classified as "permanently"
employed. By neglecting their essential needs in education,
Anglos have locked them into a vicious circle of ignorance (by
Anglo standards), which causes unemployability, which causes poverty, which causes lack of quality education, which causes ignorance. Those few young people who do manage to
break out of the circle and then try to call attention to it risk
being treated as agitators.

More often than not, these young people aggravate the
cultural dissension, which plagues the villages as an inevitable
result of contact with an overwhelmingly dominant, techno-
logically sophisticated, affluent Anglo society. They add their
considerable weight to the forces for change. They bring to

the pueblos some of the values of Anglo society—its competitiveness, its materialism, its emphasis on the individual as opposed to family or group, and its devotion to rule by majority vote as opposed to consensus reached through deliberation. They are the radicals within the village as well as outside, pressing their conservative elders to break the shell of tradition and join the twentieth century. The elders, who don't find the twentieth century all that attractive (and who usually have a vested interest in the status quo), instinctively resist. Factions develop, and the village becomes polarized. And it tends to stay that way. Changes are introduced at a glacial pace, partly because the younger people urging them generally have jobs outside the village and don't have the time required for positions of village leadership.

Because this is a frustrating situation for young people to be in, it is a wonder that so many of them continue to live in the villages. Some, of course, do not. They join the Anglo society on its own terms, working and living in town, returning occasionally to the village for nothing more than brief family visits or sporadic participation in some of the ceremonies. Yet many of these expatriates, discouraged by feelings of alienation from the land their ancestors inhabited for centuries, eventually come back to live at home, where their hearts are. Their return further intensifies the cultural split, within themselves as well as within the community.

Today a large percentage of Pueblo students are college bound. Though this might appear to be a positive sign, the competitive nature of college life comes in direct conflict with the noncompetitive social structure of Pueblo society. For the vast majority of young villagers the problems of cultural accommodation are even more acute and frustrating. Most villages have television, which injects a persistent presentation of Anglo values, the foundation of which is an obsession with possessions, in contrast with the Pueblo value system. Stressing the importance of possessions to the helplessly dispossessed creates a misery of longing and erodes Pueblo harmony in family and community life. Together with other varieties of interference, it encourages escape into the anesthetic refuge of drugs and drunkenness.

In addition to the natural problems of cultural shock, the Pueblo have had to cope with artificial problems of government interference. As many small businessmen today attest, not many things in life are more burdensome than federal paternalism. The Pueblos have been putting up with the bureaucratic paternalism of the Bureau of Indian Affairs for several generations. The treatment has been the inevitable result of setting up an agency with great authority and little accountability. Those whom it governs, or supervises, are subjects rather than constituents. Under the circumstances, it has no particular motivation to listen to them. In 1928, a scathing congressional investigative report described the Bureau's dealings with Native Americans as inadequate and unjust, adding that its neglect and mistreatment of those for whom it had been established was due at least partly to incompetence and corruption at every level. The Bureau remained unruffled. The health programs that it administered, for instance, continued to be unsatisfactory until 1954, when they were transferred by Congress to the U.S. Public Health Service, to the considerable benefit of Native Americans everywhere.

The Bureau recognizes that the two overriding problems of Pueblos—education and employment—are closely related. Over half its yearly budget is spent on education, and much of the rest on employment activities. However, it has been consistently charged with failure to spend this money effectively, allegedly because it has failed to listen, or has only half-listened, to the ideas of the people on whom the money is spent. Lately, however, the BIA/Office of Indian Education Programs has been forced to have consultation hearings twice a year on proposed changes in education with tribes at six selected sites nationwide, including Alaska. It has been making significant strides in raising the quality of education. Besides elementary schools, there are secondary schools, undergraduate scholarship programs, and programs for graduate schools and law schools.

Anglo ideas of education for Pueblos have left a great deal to be desired. Their emphasis has been on vocational training. Although this training has benefited some individuals, Pueblo leaders and Anglo allies attest that it does not address the basic, underlying education problem. That problem is one of linguistics.

Today over 400,000 Indian children attend the state public schools. About 43,000 attend Bureau of Indian Affairs schools. Most of the children entering Bureau schools do not speak English. They speak their native tongues, and some may speak a bit of Spanish. Therefore, because of English's second-language status, it should be treated as such and offered as a foreign language in school, rather than as an integral part of the Pueblo environment or as a developmental part of their learning process since birth. This seems obvious enough, yet Pueblo children continue to receive the same instruction in the basic skills of reading and writing as Anglo children of the same age group. Further, they receive this instruction in segregated schools, disallowing them the opportunity to acquire some of the language informally from contact with Anglo children. (Those enrolled in integrated public schools consistently outperform the students in Bureau schools.) Most of them struggle to learn the language, but before long discouragement sets in, then despair, then the resentful lethargy that confirms a teacher's false assumption of Indian inferiority, and finally their own conviction of the same. This incompetence in English carries over, naturally enough, into all other subject areas, because a child isn't likely to learn anything well when he or she doesn't understand the primary language. By and large, this educational system has proven to be frustrating for all concerned. It has failed to give Native American children any encouragement to master the language, or even much opportunity to do so. The children emerge from schools largely inarticulate by Anglo standards, which are the models by which they are being judged. As a result, whatever their natural skills, whatever their innate intelligence, Pueblo children are generally ill prepared to compete in the dominant culture.

Linguistic techniques have been developed for teaching English as a foreign language. Unfortunately, what is lacking more often than not is the teachers' knowledge of the children's native tongue. These and similarly helpful pedagogical devices have been slow to penetrate the governing echelons of the Bureau of Indian Affairs. Colleges of education have lagged in training teachers to handle linguistic problems and to teach English as a foreign language. As a result, both Bureau and local school systems have largely been unable to meet Indian as well as Hispanic children's needs in this respect. When the Gallup, New Mexico, public school system bit the bullet and instituted a foreign-language system for teaching English to Navajo children in first grade, neither the state universities nor the Bureau's Division of Education could provide any materials for the effort. Fortunately, the Gallup educators seem to have sturdy bootstraps.

Indeed, the general neglect of "the basics" in most schools of education, and consequently in most of the nation's schoolrooms, has aggravated the problem for children to whom English is essentially a second language. As the pendulum swings away from this neglect, greater attention may be paid to the difficulties of these children. Some states seem to be in the vanguard of this movement—notably California, Texas, and Florida. Florida especially has blazed some promising trails in recent years with its program for teaching English to children of Cuban refugees.

The failure to teach English adequately largely accounts for the failure of the Bureau's Adult Vocational Program. Naturally referred to as the AVP, it affects only about a tenth of the Pueblo population between the ages of eighteen and thirty-five. The Bureau underwrites the cost of the program for the individuals taking the training, including a subsistence allowance for themselves and their families if they are married. When the training is completed, it offers the trainee aid and counsel in seeking employment and in adjusting to life outside the reservation. But the records indicate that only about a quarter of the trainees successfully make the adjustment; the rest return discouraged to their villages.

Another result of the failure to listen seems to have been too little recognition of the great attachment of Pueblos to their home communities. Their family ties are much stronger than those of the increasingly mobile Anglo society, in which parents and their grown children often are separated by hundreds and even thousands of miles. Of the many reasons given by AVT trainees for returning home—low wages, the high cost of city living, the difficulty of adjusting to the tyranny of the clock, the petty and not so petty humiliations of discrimination—by far the most common is homesickness. This means not only that they feel at home in their communities but also that they do not feel at home in their Anglo environments. Awkwardness in speaking, writing, and understanding the language can hardly be expected to promote any other feeling.

In regard to Indian unemployment, one solution has been to encourage industries to set up factories on Pueblo land, providing residents with job opportunities while permitting them to continue living at home. Since 1957 the Bureau has had a Branch of Industrial Development that encourages such industrial decisions, although its chief effort has been in the development of tourist and recreational facilities. A heartening example of how to successfully employ Native Americans was furnished by a company that established a factory in the Rio Grande area. The official in charge of employment deliberately recruited employees from the villages on the assumption that the most promising candidates among other minorities would already have been hired by other companies. As he put it, he wanted heads, not just hands. From among the applicants he chose those who demonstrated the greatest skills in English and mathematics, combined with a willingness to learn. These characteristics, he felt, were more important than any other particular vocational training they may have received. (As industrial training consultants know, this is a very common attitude among employers.) Further, he was not distracted by the stereotype of Indian inferiority or driven by a concern to "help them overcome their cultural handicaps." On the contrary, he respected their culture and encouraged them to take pride in their background. Evidently, without being overbearing or troublesome, he cultivated their friendship on the job and got to know each employee personally, as an individual—a much acclaimed but much neglected prerequisite for a healthy business operation. While other employers complained of poor attendance records among their Native American employees, he had no absenteeism problems. His success rate may have been due to the fact that he recognized his employees' need to take time off for their religious ceremonies and for family and village business and modified the company's vacation plan to accommodate them.

Because such employers are rare, the industrial program has been inching along sluggishly at best. In very recent years the Economic Opportunity Act has been a source of hope for Native Americans, because it has given them opportunities to get out from under the paternalism of the Bureau of Indian Affairs—a paternalism, incidentally, that is slowly being eroded by outside forces. Native Americans have submitted a number of proposals, and it is significant that they are emphasizing the need of preschool education for young children, with special attention to the teaching of English. This time, apparently, Anglos are beginning to listen.

From 1933 to 1945, the Bureau was headed by a remarkable commissioner named John Collier, a perceptive, sensitive, sympathetic man who was much too intelligent and broad-minded to accept prevailing manifest-destiny notions of "inferior" cultures. Collier tried valiantly to correct misinformed perceptions of Native Americans. His own attitude is summed up in a statement included in one of his program proposals. Genuine career people in the Bureau, he wrote, "would presume—accurately—a high, not low, intelligence quotient in the Pueblo; a large, not small, capacity for discriminative and integrative thinking and for social invention; and a great, not petty, destiny as members of mankind."

He left the Bureau in 1945, a discouraged man, because he had not been able to refocus its orientation, and he had little hope that it would change in the future. But he was an idealist, measuring his effectiveness against an impossible ideal. He became discouraged because he was so far ahead of his time. Actually, John Collier's influence was considerable. The Bureau's passion for unmitigated "Americanization" has noticeably cooled, and it seems to be developing a measure of respect for the tolerant pluralism that he advocated. Although some tribes questioned his decisions, such as the reduction of sheep herds on the Navajo reservation, without John Collier's influence, Native Americans might never have seen the current revival of their ceremonial life.

That revival owes its existence also to the partial sovereignty that Native Americans enjoy within the boundaries of their reservations. That sovereignty has permitted the chief priests and the elders to reassert their authority in the villages, to reintroduce some degree of religious uniformity, and to protect the secrecy of the sacred ceremonies. Indeed, the discipline imposed in this respect is probably harsher than it ever was in previous times, when it consisted almost entirely of public ridicule. In those times each village functioned with a high degree of isolation, and the uniformity arose from a natural, instinctive kind of behavior that could be enforced, when enforcement was needed, with a very light touch. Today, amid the pressures from an enveloping and dynamically different society and the ferment of new ideas, harsher discipline has sometimes been required, including exile from the village. In a few cases, villagers who deliberately sold ceremonial secrets have been executed as traitors. So far as is known, such extreme measures were unheard of in ancient Pueblo cultures, because religion then did not have to be protected against violent interference.

Today the ceremonies range across a broad spectrum, from the very sacred and very secret to the completely secular and completely public. The most sacred and secret are the rituals of the clown and the medicine sodalities, which are conducted in a very rigid secrecy and are restricted to members of the specific sodalities. Religious kachina dances, though nearly

147

always performed in the privacy of a kiva, may be attended by any or all of the villagers; when performed outside the kiva, their privacy is protected by roadblocks and by sentinels who imperiously, yet politely, wave away any curious visitors. Ceremonies involving sacred masks, which earlier foreigners zealously destroyed and banned as works of the devil, are especially guarded from the eyes of strangers.

Somewhat less sacred and secret are community ceremonies such as those generally known to outsiders as corn dances. Preparations for these ceremonies are conducted secretly in the kivas, but the ceremonies themselves consist of public dances in the plaza, open to the eyes but not the cameras of the touring public. To some extent these dances arose as a concession to foreign meddling, ordinarily being held on the village "saint's day," in honor of San Juan, Santa Clara, and others. Kachina masks once were worn but were eliminated as a gesture of appeasement.

Still less sacred and secret are ceremonies associated with the defense of the village and with the hunt. They also are prepared for in secret but performed in public. They include war dances and animal dances in honor of the many creatures that have provided Pueblos with food and clothing for centuries: deer, antelope, buffalo, and even the snake. Many of these ceremonies originated with the nomadic hunters of the plains. The costumes associated with these ceremonies include cloth and ornaments of foreign manufacture and reveal some Hispanic and Anglo influences, however superficial.

Finally, there are ceremonies which are basically profane in character. Open to just about anybody, they are conducted chiefly as entertainments. Unlike other rituals, these are not carried out in rigid conformance with an age-old set of precise directions and are garnished with impromptu innovations

(A) Girl, dressed in traditional clothing, and two young marines (B) attend a contemporary powwow

149

during their performance. They often include mimicry of visiting tourists, although the ridicule is usually too subtle and esoteric to be offensive. Appropriately, these dances generally are performed during the Christmas holidays.

The ban on photography has been lifted in quite a few of the villages for these secular ceremonies, and some villages have relaxed it also for the war and animal dances. Pueblos have gradually come to realize that camera-snapping is an essential ingredient in the religion of tourism and also to discover that visitors are willing to pay good money for the privilege. Today this harmless addiction is a minor but quite reliable source of supplementary income.

Smaller, private ceremonies are conducted in observance of life's benchmarks: the birth of a child, the entry of a child into adulthood, marriage, and of course death. These are essentially secret; the native names of children, for instance, ordinarily are not revealed to outsiders. Christian names, such as Juan, Maria, Pedro, or Rose, have been accepted without suffering any serious identity crisis. Concurrent with native rituals, the villagers participate in Christian—mostly Catholic —ceremonies, particularly in connection with the sacraments of baptism, confirmation, matrimony, and extreme unction. Upon the death of a loved one, the bereaved often hold a ceremony of Spanish origin that would be familiar to anyone who has ever attended an Irish wake. Many people attend mass on Sundays, with various degrees of constancy and fervor, and many of their homes are decorated with images and pictures of Catholic saints. On occasion, a kind of vigil is held overnight to pray for the favor of a special saint; neighboring Hispanos often are invited to join in the ritual, which usually ends with a festive breakfast in the early morning.

This is by no means the only ceremony in which Hispanos participate. They attend mass in the villages and fraternize freely during the celebrations of saints' days, Christmas, Easter, All Souls' Day, and some other major holy days. Indeed, the survival of these ceremonies, at which Hispanos not infrequently outnumber Pueblos, may be due mainly to

Hispano participation. Indian leaders in these rituals are not the traditional Pueblo priests but rather civil authorities holding offices inherited from the reign of Governor Oñate. Pueblos, whose religion has never been afflicted with the fever of ideological certitude, seem willing to pay their respects to both religions, somewhat like modern Caucasians who pay premiums to two health-insurance companies. Without continued Hispano influence, however, they might well have returned completely to their own religion.

Part of this phenomenon of religious symbiosis, of course, has been the durability of the institution of the resident Catholic priest. The institution has had its setbacks, although the radical surgery performed during the Pueblo revolt of 1680 has never been repeated. Willa Cather, in her splendid *Death Comes for the Archbishop,* tells a story of a nineteenth-century priest at Acoma who became so obnoxious that the villagers in desperation finally threw him bodily off the cliff. And as late as around 1970 the Isleta tribal leaders handcuffed their pastor and escorted him forcibly, and permanently, out of their village. In general, however, the institution has endured in relative peace while many a clerical eye has grown weary with winking at the unorthodox shenanigans about which nothing, but absolutely nothing, could be done.

In matters political as well as religious, Pueblo society is a mixed bag. The European remodelers of the seventeenth century had tried to dismantle the age-old political structure of the Pueblos and to replace it with a European arrangement, complete with European standards. But they succeeded only in hastily applying the latter over the former, with a little dovetailing in between. Ever since, Pueblo government has been a double-layered combination, often uncomfortable but generally serviceable, and one more example of Pueblo adaptability.

The Pueblo system, still more religious than political, remains essentially the same as that described early in this book. Final authority is vested in the lifetime office of chief priest, although a council of other priests and elders can remove the incumbent in extreme cases. (The chief priests are called *caciques* by outsiders and by Pueblos conversing with them. Interestingly, the term is a native Caribbean word that the Spanish brought with them to New Mexico.) The chief priest's authority is primarily religious, but major secular decisions are brought to him for approval by the village's secular officials, whom he appoints for their limited terms. A few villages have two chief priests who alternate in office every six months (winter and summer). Membership in the village's medicine sodality is ordinarily a prerequisite for holding office.

The chief priest is always treated deferentially—except perhaps in the rare instance of impeachment, and even then depending on the reason for it. He is not to be bothered with mundane problems but must be left free for absorption in spiritual concerns. Petty quarrels are not to be brought to him, but in serious controversies he is the court of last resort. Important problems are brought to him by the tribal council. Through them, he coordinates all ceremonial and community functions. He is remote, but concerned; exalted, but solicitous; powerful, but conscientious.

The political, or civil, offices normally include those of governor, lieutenant governor, and sheriff. Significantly, one of the prerequisites for holding office is *non*membership in any of the ceremonial sodalities. Another civil office, added after the 1680 revolt, is that of war captain, which proved very important in expeditions against the Navajos and Apaches. In later years these war captains, deprived of their positions, have become ceremonial police chiefs, responsible to the chief priest for maintaining the purity of the rubrics in performance and for encouraging, sometimes enforcing, participation. This seems to have increased, rather than diminished their importance in Pueblo community life as the chief priests' men.

Regarding Pueblo civil government the present tense is not very reliable. This is the side of village life most open to outside influences, and it is in a state of agitated flux, with each pueblo experimenting with its own mix of innovations and traditions. In some villages the chief priests' secular wings have been clipped by the introduction of elections, so that the governor and lieutenant governor are more directly answerable to the people. Another Anglo-inspired innovation has been the elected tribal council. Still another is the salary paid to the governor, making the office more desirable and prestigious, and permitting the incumbent to devote himself to it full-time. Finally, there is woman suffrage. In 1974 a small village north of Santa Fe elected a young woman to the governorship, spinning bodies in countless ancient graves. In the eighties, Isleta also elected a woman to two terms as governor. Like most outside innovations, these have caused some pushing and pulling between the standpatters and the would-be pace-setters. Since the spirit of the times is with the latter, Pueblos are likely to see considerable change in their political arrangements for some years to come.

They are not so likely to see any significant change in their ancient religion. By and large, they are committed to it. Although evangelical Christianity has taken hold among some Native Americans of the plains, the Pueblos of the Southwest seem inclined to preserve the traditional communion between nature and the human spirit, even if others claim that something better has come along.

BIBLIOGRAPHY

Bolton, Herbert E. *Coronado, Knight of Pueblos and Plains.* Albuquerque: University of New Mexico Press, 1949.

Collier, John. *Indians of the Americas.* New York: American Library, 1947.

Dozier, Edward P. *The Pueblo Indians of America.* New York: Holt, Rinehart and Winston, 1970.

Estabrook, Emma. *Givers of Life: The American Indians as Contributors to Civilization.* Albuquerque: University of New Mexico Press, 1931.

Fergusson, Erna. *New Mexico, A Pageant of Three Peoples.* New York: Alfred A. Knopf, 1966.

Hackett, Charles Wilson. *Revolt of the Pueblo Indians.* Albuquerque: University of New Mexico Press, 1942.

Hewett, Edgar Lee. *Ancient Life in the American Southwest.* New York: Biblo and Tannen, 1968.

Horgan, Paul. *Great River: The Rio Grande in North American History.* New York: Rinehart & Co., 1954.

Jones, Oakah L., Jr. *Pueblo Warriors and the Spanish Conquest.* Norman: University of Oklahoma Press, 1966.

Ryan, J. C. *Revolt Along the Rio Grande.* San Antonio: The Naylor Company, 1964.

Silverberg, Robert. *The Pueblo Revolt.* New York: Weybright and Talley, 1970.

Smith, Anne M. *New Mexico Indians: Economic, Educational and Social Problems.* Santa Fe: Museum of New Mexico, 1966.

Spicer, Edward H. *Cycles of Conquest.* Tucson: University of Arizona Press, 1962.

Terrell, John Upton. *Pueblos, Gods and Spaniards.* New York: Dial Press, 1973.

Tyler, Hamilton A. *Pueblo Gods and Myths.* Norman: University of Oklahoma Press, 1964.

Walters, Frank. *Masked Gods: Navaho and Pueblo Ceremonialism.* Albuquerque: University of New Mexico Press, 1950.

INDEX